More than a Housewife
Talent! Purpose! Direction! Drive!

VICKI GUNVALSON

With Jeff Scott

More Than a Housewife

Woo-Hoo Productions, LLC
P.O. Box 500
Trabuco Canyon, CA 92678

First Published in Rancho Santa Margarita, Ca. 2009
by Woo-Hoo Productions

10 9 8 7 6 5 4 3 2 1

Library of Congress Control Number — 2009939933

ISBN 978-0-615-32490-6

1. Biographical 2. Inspirational 3.Business

Cover Design by: kim@kimsawyerdesign.com
Photography by: www.ericnelsonphotography.com
Writing by: Jeff Scott (jscott@tdoent.com)

250 - 18Dec09

More than a Housewife

Talent! Purpose! Direction! Drive!

To my father, William J. Steinmetz,
for teaching by example and showing me
that through perseverance, anything is possible.
To my mother, Joanne,
for her continued love and faithfulness.

MORE THAN A HOUSEWIFE

Contents

Forward
By
Jeff Scott

Though I enjoy writing self-help fiction stories, occasionally I ghostwrite for business professionals. The projects that appeal to me most are those that offer value to the reader. Oftentimes, I'll receive pages of material with a message out of context. There've been times where I'm given material that could be considered the "meat" of the book, but it lacks a beginning and an end.

When writing for a client, their personality traits are revealed to me and I begin to understand what they're really all about, deep within. This is where I begin creating content that comes across to the reader in the voice of the one for whom I write.

I interviewed Vicki for many hours and with thousands of questions. Taking the information to my office and deciphering exactly how to write the material in her voice, becomes the game.

If there is any one word that I would use to describe Vicki Gunvalson, it would be "tenacious." In Webster's dictionary, the word is defined as: "not easily pulled apart; Cohesive, Tough (as in metal)."

Many people have viewed Vicki throughout each season of The Real Housewives of Orange County, and from the research I've done, the viewers have mixed feelings about the show and the personalities.

I went out on the town to create conversations with people regarding TV reality shows. Many people swear they don't watch "reality" TV, yet I'm always amazed to find that they know of the OC housewives and which women they gravitate toward, or, just the opposite, are repulsed by.

Through these conversations, I find that most people can list five or more reality show themes... cooking, housewives, fighting, modeling, designing, survival, cops and more. I question whether these same people would deny slowing down to observe an accident on the freeway.

When it comes to the OC Housewives, I would hope the public in Orange County and around the rest of the nation would stop for a moment and think before believing that these women of reality are threatening or gossiping about each other 24/7. I tend to find that's been the viewer's job.

I also hope a viewer as far away as Oshkosh doesn't get the idea that everyone in the OC is contagious with reality fever.

Regarding Vicki, I found her to be very forthcoming and open with anything that was asked of her. Through the book, we included questions coming straight from the fans via Vicki's Facebook site. There were a few derogatory comments, but for the most part, many respectable questions coming from inquiring minds.

I approached Vicki through a friend and asked if she was interested in writing a book. As it turned out, she was already in the process, but wasn't happy with what was being written. Since I knew her personality and background from the TV show, I instantly knew what to say and what she was about.

Growing up with my sister in a single parent household, my mother worked two jobs to make ends meet. I could empathize with Vicki's demeanor when it comes to her controlling personality. When a woman does not get support either mentally, physically or monetarily from her spouse, such as my mother went through, the woman will begin to change her mode of operation. At this point the thought is — sink or swim! Like my mother, Vicki decided to swim ... and then some.

Through the interviews, I realized that Vicki had put this mode of operation in her mind and will never relent on what she thinks is the right thing to do. Though Vicki did eventually marry a very stable man, Donn Gunvalson, and thought she could relax a little, once the mind is programmed through an emotional charge, there is rarely a way to turn back or ever relinquish complete control to anyone.

This book represents Vicki in a different light, but not all that far from the woman you see on TV. Show after show, people are referring to her work habits and extolling their ideas that she needs to slow down. Please feel free to take notes when I tell you that she can't slow down. To do so would take her to a place she doesn't want to go. She is so used to performing at an extremely fast pace and with exorbitant amounts of energy that it has become normal to her existence. To take that ability away from her would be like asking Einstein to teach the theory of relativity to a group in a mental ward — a real waste of talent.

Over the years I've had quite a few personal experiences of people just like Vicki. I've watched them build their businesses and never take much time for themselves. I've noticed that the faster they work, and the more they demand from others, mountains begin to move. They don't have time to stop and smell the roses, nor do they want or need to. Their dreams are diligently materialized quickly by the sheer fact that they're innovators, and if someone says something to the effect of, "That's just the way it is," these innovators prove otherwise.

At the other end of the spectrum, I see the people that start a small business, wanting for financial success, but can't bring themselves to action. They worry about failure and oftentimes focus more on finding a job, and being safe, than to take the next step toward financial success. Most of Vicki's success has been through taking risks and working the long hours that others just won't voluntarily accept as part of the process.

In person, I found Vicki to be very pleasant and from the first time we met she talked with me as though we'd been friends forever. Through my questions, I found that she is genuinely concerned about others, and though the TV show rarely, if ever, depicts that side of her, I assure you it does exist.

I see Vicki as an inspiration to many. As a matter of fact, the theme of this book was not supposed to be just about her life on TV. She was quite deliberate when we crossed our thoughts on what she should express through this book. First, she wanted it to be easily understood. We've done this through the use of a few metaphors. Second, she wanted to let single parents, men and women, know that they too can create a greater lifestyle for their families. Third, she wanted to express that the TV show doesn't reflect the whole person that she has become. Through watching herself and her actions, she has grown.

In business, Vicki exceeds expectations on a daily basis in an industry run mainly by men. The housewives across the country that sit at home and watch their soap operas don't understand someone like Vicki; all the while, men are quick to acknowledge her accomplishments. She confronts life head on and her dialogue is often a reflection of how deeply rooted in business she is. She won't beat around the bush when it comes to what she wants. Again, it's sink or swim.

In a final thought about Vicki, I believe she will become an inspiration to many throughout the coming years. She will refine herself as she has done her business, but I also believe that when she does refine and focus her energy, she will eventually ride a wave that leads to the success of not only herself, but many of those connected to her. I know this will actually come to fruition since she is definitely spot-on purpose.

I read a fun fact that stated 95% of material read in a self-help book is not retained by the reader, but over 85% of fictional stories are. I hope you will understand that this book is kept simple through the use of metaphors or shared personal experiences. They're to be used to figure out one's own situations in life and to possibly spark new ideas or understandings of how some things may work.

FORWARD

Vicki's goal through this book is to help or inspire those who want more from life. My goal through this book is to help her make that possible.

Jeff Scott

MORE THAN A HOUSEWIFE

Introduction
By
Vicki Gunvalson

I originally started out with the idea of writing a book like every other woman of the Bravo Housewives series, but then I thought I might have more to say than who was doing what to whom and how life just isn't fair. Now, my objective through this book is to help empower people that might be searching for a different direction in life.

It's not that I can solve everyone's problems, not by a long shot, but what I can do is to show you where I come from and how I kept my life together through some very difficult times. Hopefully, this will help others to realize that they too can make positive strides.

If you notice the sections of the book listed in contents, you'll see that I start out with "Transformations." I'm not the first to transform my life, but transforming is something we all do, almost day in and day out.

While working with a writer and through hours of answering questions, we put together some of the basics of my life, but also, some of the most relevant obstacles and triumphs I've experienced.

I tend to think that my biggest audience for this book will be women, but I don't want to shortchange men by saying there is nothing in the book for them, and that they wouldn't be interested. There are plenty of men in the world with open minds that have learned valuable lessons from a woman (think in terms of mom). Perhaps, the latest information they may accept is that business is not just a man's game in the 21st century.

My goal is to help empower those with an open mind and that believe in possibilities, regardless if it's a man, woman or child.

While working on this book, many things became distinctly clear. I'd been on purpose throughout my life, but wasn't as fully aware of it as I am now. When you learn how I recognized my purpose, you too, may begin to focus in on yours.

I started with the basics: my childhood. I then continued with a few experiences in my young adult life. When I came to the point of my first and only divorce, I began to really focus on what I wanted to do and what I was drawn to. At this point, I had to make command decisions and use the family drive, the alter ego that says "MOVE FOR-WARD!"

After I began a career in life insurance, the first time, I was finally making decisions and putting definitive order in my life. What often happens when putting order in your life? Chaos will rear its ugly head. I share what I learned to do when life begins to unravel or become unbalanced.

Through what seems like synchronicity, Donn Gunvalson, came back into my life and we became the couple that we should have been from the start. When we married and moved to California I thought I'd hit the jackpot. I was going to be the stay-at-home mom and raise the all-American family like the infamous Ozzie and Harriett Nelson.

Once again, through circumstances that I wasn't happy with, I had to transform. Donn and I share similar family backgrounds (our parents married for life) that said, "Stick it out," or "Make it work," and that's just what we've done. This is not to say that times haven't been tough or very trying for us, but through our Mid-western values we have managed to work things out.

In Section Two I discuss the challenges I experienced when first starting my business; what it took to raise my courage level, and then as described in contents, break through and break away. Never have my experiences led me to live a simple, run-of-the-mill and effortless existence.

In Section Three, I cover the idea that I'm a celebrity.

INTRODUCTION

Sure, I'm well known since the show The Real Housewives of Orange County became a hit, but celebrity? I'll save that title for the day I get paid 20 million to promote a product like the real stars, excuse me … the "real" celebrities.

Do I like the attention of celebrity? Sure. I was a popular girl when I was younger and the circumstances behind that popularity afforded me the opportunity to share with my friends. I ended Section Three, "The Experience, Overall," because people have often asked me why I chose to do this type of reality show. I think one might have a different perspective after reading the answer.

When it comes to the last section, I share my personal thoughts and philosophies on different topics. You may notice that the last chapter is titled, "Maturing a Life, Completing the Puzzle." This is mostly about how I have come full circle with each stage of my life, personal and business.

I won't be retiring any time soon as there are many people that depend on me daily to manage their insurance and retirement needs. There is a tremendous amount of pressure to make sure when I tell someone that their money will grow and be available when they retire, it had better have done just that. If I promise them that upon the death of a loved one, their policy will pay them the death benefit as it was designed to do, I'd better be right.

Once again, through this book, I wish to reach out to those who are wondering how, they too, can make a better life. I'm not a perfect person, but I am an excellent transformer. I wish you the best and hope you enjoy reading my story.

Vicki Gunvalson

MORE THAN A HOUSEWIFE

Section One

Transformations

MORE THAN A HOUSEWIFE

Chapter One

Childhood

Reflections of the Past

While waiting for the camera crews to set up, I'll sometimes take a stroll around the room and think about what I've been involved in. For the past five years I've had so many people make comments regarding my part on the show. Some hate me, others love me. Some are inspired by my business sense and others loath how my husband and I interact. I would hope that most of the viewing audience understands the real "reality" of it all.

The filming is soon to start and though we're never supposed to mention the camera while shooting, if one woman gets angry with another, there've been times you want to tell the crew to stop filming unless they're going to follow us outside.

It's during these moments of badgering between the ladies that I sometimes want to break-out in tears. They're not physically hurting me, but there is something that gets my emotions riled and I begin to cry.

I really dislike this part of the experience and it often makes me reflect on my past. Growing up in a house with the majority being women, you'd think I'd be used to the hormonal influx of attitudes, but nothing can prepare you for the wretchedness of women living in a high-priced society under the guise that they're self-made. I came from a solid family life and never knew such cruelty existed, until I didn't become a part of the cutting room floor.

Some of the women from previous seasons, including me, have had differences of opinions, but this is not to reflect that all the women are downright fiendish. I've noticed over the years, each new season has introduced a younger group of women and the verbal inflictions have increased tremendously.

Many times, after a day of filming, I'll find my way to the car and sit for a moment while crying. I tell myself time and again, "This is not normal for me," yet the tears keep flowing.

Someone once told me that tears come from our past. We subconsciously recognize an earlier incident in life and if it has enough emotion attached to it, and we can associate it with what's happening in the present, we can't help but to break-down and emit those same exact emotions over and over again. The only way to stop the cycle is to understand what one is attached to — a study of the previous incident. Slowly, I began to think of the worst scenarios of my life. Though there weren't many, the ones that I did recognize were significant.

In this book, I can't and won't go through my life day by day because this would just bore you to death. I will share the times that either meant the most to me or helped create the person you think you know today.

Thinking back, I realize and truly appreciate what an incredible childhood I had, but when you live in a house that's so big and beautiful and the walls come crumbling down, what do you do?

I was born into such a house with a family that was big and beautiful too. We lived the big dreams and were taught to make big things happen. One of five children, I've never once been allowed to believe that I was incapable of great things.

My father, William Steinmetz, was born in 1930. My grandfather, a stunning man in his own right, must have taught my father the confidence and desire to succeed he

14

eventually showered upon my siblings and me. He was a stern man that demanded respect within his family and could command the moment with a single glance. This is not to say my father was bereft of compassion. He cared dearly for his family and would see to it that each of his children learned and understood that a good work ethic was somehow superior to a college education. We understood that this work ethic would take us as far as we wanted to go in life.

I would dare to say that my father bestowed a legacy that I've adhered to through the strength of his example. It has become imbedded in my subconscious.

My childhood was never a simple measure of time. I prevailed through many life-altering experiences a child should never endure. Before I get ahead of myself, let me go back to where it all started.

My parents, William and Joanne, met at a carnival. My father was being set up with another woman, but by the end of the evening, on the drive home, he maneuvered himself into the back seat to make sure he was next to my mother. One and a half years later, in1952, they were married.

Trying to conceive their first child proved to be difficult. After five years of marriage they decided to adopt twins Kathy and Kim, who were babies, born in 1957 and brought into the Steinmetz home.

In those days, having one or two kids would be just the beginning for growing a family in the Midwest. Ten years after my parents married and five years after bringing the twins home, they were still trying to conceive a child of their own. My mother began visiting fertility doctors and doing anything she could to conceive. It wasn't necessarily out of desperation; she just wanted to have a child of her own.

I came along, somewhat unexpectedly, in 1962. All the waiting, the fertility doctors, the procedures, nothing seemed to be working. Then there I was and incredibly, 13 months later my sister Lisa. In another four years, our family became complete when Billy (William), the first boy, was born.

Though I'm close to all of my siblings, the twins were five years ahead of me and Billy was five years behind. Lisa is the one I tend to gravitate toward the most and with whom I share a psychic closeness. When she is feeling down about something, I will know it before she tells me. We're so close that it almost seems as if we're the twins of the family. Today, we're in the same line of work, and if we fly to meet somewhere, we'll both come off the plane wearing almost identical outfits.

I have fond childhood memories of Lisa and even our little spats were playful: "Stay out of my closet!" or "Who said you could wear my clothes?"

There were no knock-down, drag-out fights in my family. Who could face THE look from my father if he found out there was civil unrest in HIS peaceful household?

When I was just five years old, I was diagnosed with a non-cancerous cholesteatoma. This is a very rare condition that begins to eat the three small bones located in the middle ear. If undetected or left untreated, it can produce enzymes that will affect and possibly erode the thin bone structure that separates the brain from the top of the ear. It can also spread a serious infection to the thin-coated veil of the brain, leading to very serious complications.

When I underwent my first operation at seven, I remember my mother was crying hysterically, wondering if I was going to die. Every few years, I go in for an operation that keeps the benign tumor at bay. The surgeons relieved my symptoms but didn't cure me. As a child, I was always fearful of the next operation. Even though they were all successful, each one was scary and there always seemed to be another one looming.

I remember coming home from the hospital the very first time with bandages wrapped all around my head. Though I did get preferential treatment from my parents and siblings, I don't believe my sisters ever objected to picking up behind me or doing my chores. As mentioned earlier, we really did get along very well and the twins just seemed to understand that it was their place to look out for me since I was so much younger. Perhaps, their kindness came from my father, through them.

Whatever the case, my older sisters are, to this day, still very compassionate. Their ways are their own, and in manner and bearing, they are different from Lisa, my brother and me. Kathy and Kim were both very athletic, tomboys. Not me, I'm far from athletic.

My sister Kim might have been considered socially awkward, but her sports skills were exceptional. She was one of my father's favorites. Her great athleticism made it possible for her to become one of the first recipients of a college scholarship for women's basketball. When she was younger, she could bump and check with the toughest hockey players around and my father enjoyed every bit of this. Though Billy was quite an athlete himself, Kim was the star in my father's eyes.

Never truly comfortable in her skin, because of her large frame or what some might consider masculine features, Kim was very much a woman with deep-seated, unanswered questions. While away at college, in her third year, Kim decided to do the unthinkable. One night, she wrote out a note informing the family that she just wasn't happy with herself and didn't like what she saw in the mirror. Then she jumped out of an 8th floor dormitory window to end her life.

In a harsh and cold November night, Kim lay for six hours before someone found her body and immediately she was medevaced to the nearest hospital. She was still alive. My family rushed to her side. The first doctor with whom my parents spoke refused to operate on her since she had tried to kill herself. My guess was that he thought he was wasting his time. If only he knew her now.

The second doctor was an Army surgeon and he sympathized with my mother and father, knowing that Kim was and is someone's daughter. This surgeon must have had kids himself and realized that children change their minds more often than their clothes and he had to save her life if he could.

Opening Kim's chest and stomach, the surgical team searched for internal damage and found nothing except some broken ribs, a fractured pelvis and a mangled arm. It was truly a miracle that she had not hit her head. God had plans for her!

She was fortunate enough to land in such a way that she was not paralyzed, that she would eventually walk again, that she was going to live! The doctors were also able to save her arm after doing several repairs and skin grafts. After spending eight months in a very intensive recovery and rehabilitation program, Kim regained complete control of her body. She managed to pull her life back together and found she wanted her second chance.

By August, she would go back to the same college, the same dorm and, thankfully, never again tried to commit suicide. From that point on, the subject was never spoken about. My mother, having read the goodbye note, tried to make sense of it all. She tried to make Kim understand that there is always going to be something we don't like about ourselves. No one will ever be perfect. Though this wisdom was directed at Kim, I tend to think I got the message.

Kim must have taken my mother's insight to heart, and though she occasionally feels pain in her limbs when the weather changes and the arthritis kicks in, I'm happy to say that she is strong and doing well 30 years later. She returned to college, received her degree in physical education and found work as a substitute gym teacher and nurse's aide for a nursing home. The social awkwardness is still prevalent. She has an easier time dealing with people that are much younger or clearly much older than her. She shies away from people her own age. Disliking doctors, dentists, psychologists or other forms of medicine, she persists in living life her way. More power to her.

As for Kathy, she too was a very athletic child, just not as gifted. As twins, she and Kim wore the same styles and developed many of the same mannerisms as they grew up. Since they were five years older than I, our social circles rarely crossed, but we were all popular enough in the neighborhood that people could place the Steinmetz name and instantly correlate the relationship. Today, Kathy is an insurance underwriter, married and plays a great game of golf.

When it comes to Lisa and me, we knew everything there was to know about each other. Being so close in age and having a tight circle of friends was a comfort. We always knew we could count on each other no matter what.

At one point during high school, my father set a curfew. Lisa and I were supposed to be in by 11:00. There were a few nights when the hour came and went and Lisa and I were not home. We always managed to piece together a good excuse. Even though my father was the strict disciplinarian, Lisa and I thought we were smart enough to make the perfect excuse. The part of the equation we always forgot, however, was that my father was always thinking ahead of us and he had THE look.

If we hadn't been so frightened by the look we would have walked all over him the way we occasionally did our mother. We crossed that look at our peril. One night Lisa and I were at the apartment of a male friend who had already graduated high school, and we were late getting home. When we did make it into the house, my father grabbed me. I could see the seriousness of his building anger. Luckily, escaping to my room before he landed too many whacks on my behind, I made it a point to never bring out that particular monster again.

In one of the many rooms Lisa and I shared, we'd huddle on the corner of a bed and we'd sometimes giggle at the thought of escaping his justice, and try to make jokes out of the consequences of incurring his full wrath.

My father provides

By the time I was in 8th grade, my father's business had grown so large and profitable that we ended up moving to a 6,000-square-foot house with six bedrooms and seven baths in Palatine, Illinois. Considered a village in Cook County, Palatine is located in a northwestern suburb of Chicago called Plum Grove Estates.

We were finally in a place where there was enough rooms to spread out and not be on top of each other. Lisa and I still shared a bedroom, but it was huge. We had a balcony which overlooked the woods just beyond our one-acre back-yard. Our boyfriends, from time to time, would climb the brick wall to sneak into our room — something our parents never knew about (even to this day!). I have amazing memories of this house, and every time I visit my family, I make it a point to drive by and reminisce.

My father had one of the largest acoustical and dry-wall construction companies in Chicago and, at one point, had about 200 people on his payroll.

Through construction and asbestos removal the business provided us an ever more prosperous lifestyle. Before moving into the Palatine house, my parents had earlier built a huge A-frame house on lakefront property in Hay-word, Wisconsin. It was perfect for long hot summers and holiday getaways.

Each of us kids could bring a friend to the summer house. It often became so packed that people were sleeping here, there and everywhere. A favorite memory will always be an evening when everyone was sitting around the fire pit. The conversations and joking were as warm as the fire. If we weren't water-skiing during the summer, then we were ice-skating on the lake or snowmobiling through the thick forests in the winter. I remember at one point think-ing that life doesn't get any better than this — or does it?

Another favorite family activity was to travel and

camp. My father would plan a summer trip for the family by unfolding a big map and having each of us kids pick a place we wanted to visit. In the beginning, we hauled a pop-up trailer and pitched tents. Then as things got better, we were hauling a self-contained camper with beds and all the amenities. Life is for the living and that's just what we did.

When times were good in the Steinmetz household, things were great. In my teens, I remember one Christmas, when, after returning home from midnight mass, we sat around the tree and proceeded to open presents. My father would try to get each of us kids something special. This year, after all the big presents were opened, there was one more present for each of us. Together, we all ripped the wrapping off a small box that fit nicely in our hands. Simultaneously, we peered into the boxes. We had each received five fresh $100 bills. I thought I was rich.

When my father could afford to be generous, he truly took care of his family and friends.

Boys and Barbies

Thinking back on good times, I was always happiest when I either had a crush on a guy or was actually involved. One of my first crushes came early and I can actually say it was also my first marriage, but of course this was just play. I was about five when Jimmy Dolan, the brother of my good friend Colleen, and I had a little wedding ceremony with reception included. My mom got me a white dress and my friend was the maid-of-honor. We strolled down a makeshift aisle. And though I don't remember who performed the ceremony, I do remember how much fun I had and how happy I was.

Colleen grew to be a life-long friend, though now we don't get the chance to talk as much as we'd like. When we do get to stroll down memory lane — games we played and the summer trips to the cabin — it always solidifies the most heartfelt friendship I have ever experienced.

In 8th grade, I had a crush on a boy named John

Graziano and I always wanted to sit next to him on the school bus, but he was more interested in my friend Carol Piper. I never made a scene over it and when I got to high school things took a turn for the better. I continued to have a strong interest in boys, and in my freshman year, I had my first serious, long-term relationship. I began seeing one of the popular boys in Fremd High School. Robert was the same age and I met him because our lockers were right next to each other. We started dating almost immediately and our relationship was the best. It was so good that even our parents were close and sometimes they joked about who was going to pay for what part of our wedding.

During our relationship, I blossomed in more ways than one. I felt I was in love and was willing to go the distance. For many women their first experience in the boudoir is not always pleasant. Through stories I've heard, it was always the boy who got his deal and then moved on, most often leaving the girl feeling used or shamed. Well, lucky me, I didn't experience that. Robert was very respectful and alone time was always special.

Most of my friends were in long-term committed relationships with their boyfriends and everyone knew each other's story — who was doing what and where it was happening. During my senior year, my friends and I would find a way to buy some alcohol, and though we never really drank a lot or got anywhere near drunk, we enjoyed ourselves and some Friday night pizza at Barrow's after the football games. Other substances were never an option, and there wasn't even a smoker of any kind in our circle of friends. That was for the other crowds.

It was almost as if we were playing parental roles; we just didn't have the complete responsibilities they did and we gossiped about our endeavors a whole lot more. Thinking back about how much was going on, I'm kind of shocked that none of my friends or me wound up rearing children before their time. All I knew was that neither of my parents where aware of my playful antics with Robert, and that was an incredibly good thing.

In my junior year, Robert started to act differently and things began to change. I remember his dropping me off from school one day and telling me that he loved me but felt it was best for us to break up, grow independently and to date other people. I was devastated but remember walking to my friend Gayle's house. In shock and hysterically crying, I was scared of being alone and had a hard time coping with this too. All of my girlfriends still had boyfriends and I was now the odd one out.

I ended up going to the dances with other class members, but always looked to see who Robert was with and what he was wearing. I wanted to get back together with him and hoped it was only a temporary break-up. Unfortunately, it wasn't.

We would stay in touch but never become a couple again. He went away to college while I stayed home. I felt stuck in Palatine. Eventually, we grew further apart and lost contact.

A few years later when I was about to get married, Robert's dad asked if I was sure about what I was doing. He informed me that Robert would be coming back from college and suggested the possibility of our getting back together. It was a tempting thought, but I knew it was completely over. No one but Robert really wanted it to be, but it was.

School

School, for me, was really more of a social gathering. I was never a great student and though I was popular, and "in" with the cheerleaders, I never made the squad. I tried, but when it came to dancing and tumbling, let's just say I had two left feet. Funny, but those two left feet walked onto the track where I'd try my best at hurdles. Can someone have two left legs too?

When it came to my course work, I'd have to say that history and government were my worst subjects. I was always interested in the present or the future and just didn't have time, or take the time, to realize the relevancy of the past.

If there was anything that I did enjoy in school, it was math. I've always been good with numbers and truly liked the challenge of solving the difficult questions in word form, you know... If two trains are on the same track one hour apart and moving at such and such speed, when will they meet? Hmm, I never really told anyone that math was a turn-on for me, but had I, who knows? Perhaps, someone would have directed me towards a career as a CPA.

In my generation, college was never a forgone conclusion, especially for girls. My father's old mindset was that girls could go to college, but most should be at home taking care of the family. He was paradoxical in his thinking, telling his kids that we are all very capable of being self-sufficient and successful, yet never quite letting go of the old notions about women being best suited to be wives and moms, not professionals or all of the above.

When high school ended and I graduated, I wasn't sure exactly what to do or what I even wanted to do. My parents never encouraged college for anyone except Billy. When I asked my dad what I should do with my life, he would ask, "What do you want to do?" I was lost.

I found myself continuing to work at the Jewel Grocery Store, paying for my own car and going to Harper Jr. College for six months. Analyzing my situation, I wasn't at all sure why I was going to college. Why a liberal arts degree? When I couldn't come up with an answer, I left.

Shortly after leaving Harper College, a friend and I enrolled in a vocational school for cosmetology, where after 1500 hours of training, I earned a certificate.

Mom

Throughout my childhood, my mother and I were very close, though I was a bit closer to my dad. She was a good mother, but I often thought that she just wasn't happy with her life. I remember when I brought friends over, I warned them ahead of time that if my mother went off on one of her tangents, we'd leave immediately. When coming home from school, I'd stop at the front door and listen carefully to hear if she was screaming about something. She didn't have Tourette's syndrome, but seemed to have more than a nodding acquaintance with the disease.

My mom had five kids and a huge house to keep clean. She was called up to task and stepped up for Kim in a semi-disabled state after her tragic suicide attempt. Life had to be hard for her.

There was no maid, no cook and no one helped her out with the household duties from washing clothes to ironing. When it came time for dinner, she set the table for us kids, and then later when my father got home from working a 10- to 12-hour day, she prepared his food and sat down to eat with him.

Thinking about it, I'm sure she was exhausted from her daily duties and it showed through, in her temperament. I was often embarrassed by her actions, but eventually came to realize that maybe she really just wasn't happy. Mind you, I did learn at least four things from her that have resonated throughout my life:

1. Dress impeccably.
2. Never scream at your kids in front of their friends.
3. Keep an orderly, clutter-free and beautifully decorated home.
4. Be a good cook and know how to sew.

I follow this advice today because of her. I've never known a mother who yelled so much, while looking so good, dressed to the nines. She looked like she was straight out of a Vogue magazine cover.

Regardless of her volume while I was growing up, we were very close, and are to this day. Though I haven't al-

25

ways shown her the respect that I gave my father, I always loved her and never wanted to disappoint either one of them.

Times got rough in my junior year when my family experienced a serious financial tragedy. After a secretary in my father's company embezzled funds, his business imploded. My father pledged our big home as collateral for a bank loan to meet payroll. When the bank called in the note, my dad couldn't repay it. The bank foreclosed on our home. Eventually, my father declared bankruptcy, and just after my senior year, we had to move.

No longer did we have the biggest house in the neighborhood and no longer were my parents welcome at the prestigious Rolling Green Country Club. I was completely and utterly embarrassed, as was my entire family. I felt that my life was over. I was no longer the girl who had it all. I wasn't a pauper, but I also wasn't the go-to-girl who hosted a lavish lifestyle for her friends.

When I look back on that whole situation, I realize I had a lot of growing up to do. I was like any other teenager — self-absorbed. Yes, the whole world revolved around me, so I wasn't particularly understanding or supportive. I was just unhappy about my circumstances. Perhaps, I needed to go through this. That experience is a part of who I was and who I became. I think it shaped my future.

I think my father was the most disappointed of us all. He truly felt like he failed my mother and his family. I don't believe she ever let him live it down. She seemed to react to our fall from grace the same way I did. She was embarrassed beyond anything she'd ever experienced. Hmm, I guess I wasn't alone. But I was a kid; she was the grown-up.

Eventually, we would have another home, though not as large, and the business would be revived. My father recouped a part of his financial loss. Still, nothing was ever quite the same. My father tried to calm my mom and to make everything up to her, but she would just lose it on many occasions. He never stopped trying to comfort her, to make it all better.

Work & Jobs

My very first job was scooping ice cream at the local Swenson's. My father bestowed on his kids a great work ethic, one so great that I adhere to it to this very day, but it started at Swenson's. When each of us kids turned 16 we got a car. At the same time my dad handed over the keys to my '77 Mustang, he also bestowed upon me a payment book. Each month I'd have to come up with roughly $180 and I found scooping ice cream wasn't covering that bill. I searched out another job and eventually ended up at Wendy's Hamburgers. Robert worked there with me, so I was fortunate to be able to see him, not only at school, but also at work. After he left Wendy's, he got a job at Jewel Grocery Store and asked me to apply there too. I quickly got an interview and was working with Robert again.

At first, I did what every other beginner does, and that was bagging groceries and collecting shopping carts. When I got the chance to move up to a clerk position, I took it. More money meant my car got paid off faster.

I actually got so good at being a clerk that I could be reading the price of an item in one hand while my other hand was punching the cash register keypad. There were no bar-code scanners in those days. My eyes were my scanners and my fingers were the input system of that era.

Jewel's computers timed us on how fast we rang up groceries and most every month, I was the winner. My name often appeared on the board in the break room as the fastest checker. I became accustomed to this acknowledgement and pushed to continue my winning streak. It was the start of my competitiveness, I was shifting into drive.

MORE THAN A HOUSEWIFE

Chapter Two

Young Adult

A Maturing Mind

The relationship with Robert ended when he broke up with me just after my junior year. I was devastated by this, but it didn't take long before I started to understand things, pick up the pieces and get back into the mix.

Soon, there would be a new boyfriend, Michael, who bagged groceries at Jewel. The three of us, Robert, Mike and I, worked together for a short time, and when word spread that Robert and I were no longer a couple, Mike made his move.

He was a nice guy, soft spoken, simple and easy to get along with. There was something about him that I should have recognized, been able to pinpoint, but more so, there was something within me that I should have known.

Mike was two years older than I and what I took for ambition, reflected in a nice car, steady job and great body, turned out to be another fantasizing moment in my life. A hot car and a nice body, oh, if I had only known this wasn't the way to pick them. You live and you learn.

Robert was off to college, so that door was completely closed. Something within me was never content with being alone. I liked the fact that Mike was a couple of years older. He made me feel special, somehow more mature and able to mix with an older crowd. My imagination really was getting the better of me and I believed everything I told myself.

Finally, while graduating high school, I remember being scared and crying, wondering what I was going to do. Some of my friends saw the paths they planned to travel, but I saw nothing. I wasn't college material, though I did attend for six months. I felt as if I were stuck. Things just weren't clicking for me, so I remained at my checkout stand and punched numbers while Mike stocked grocery shelves.

When I went to my dad again and asked him what I should do, he said, "Your mother didn't go to college and everything worked out. You could work for me in the office." That wasn't the answer I was looking for. It seemed there just wasn't any real guidance available.

Back at Jewel, Mike always made it a point to be nearby and bag groceries for me when he could. He was fun to be around. He was an athlete who played a couple years of high school football, but never had any real dreams for using football to get him to college. It seems I had over-estimated his ambition of which, at the time, mainly consisted of being a unionized stock person. I guess that was all he wanted to do, put items on the shelf and price them, click, stamp, click, stamp. I can still hear the price-sticker gun going off in my head.

Though there is nothing wrong with being a stock person, it wasn't going to lead to the lifestyle I knew I wanted to live. The warning signs were flashing.

Mike and I were together for almost two years. My parents were going through the turmoil of a ruined family business and trying to put everything back together after the bankruptcy. With the financial instability pressure, we were all on edge. One day, a battle broke out between my mother and me. We'd never before experienced a disagreement of this magnitude, and while things were still heated, I called Mike and impulsively asked him to marry me. "We could get a place and move in together," I told him.

At this point, my grandfather went to my mother and told her to stop this marriage before it even started. My mother's reply was, "She's going to do what she wants to do." Perhaps, my grandfather was wiser than anyone gave him credit for, but my mother was right - I was going to do what I wanted.

As things progressed and Mike and I became more serious about a future together, my father took him aside and told him, "If you're going to marry my daughter, you'll have to work in the family business." My dad had his suspicions of Mike not being able to provide for a family and felt he should be forced to have a career that paid well.

Even though my mother told my grandfather she was powerless to intervene, she did come forth to tell me that Mike wasn't a good fit for the family. I wasn't willing to listen to this. My immediate family didn't have faith in Mike and felt he wasn't ambitious enough for me, yet, I told them not to worry, "I think he'll become a go-getter. He'll rise to the occasion. He can become more aggressive. It'll be fine. Just wait, you'll see."

In hindsight, this was probably one of my biggest mistakes — creating an image in my mind that Mike could be something he had absolutely no desire to be.

Mike had some great qualities, but I think he let them be overshadowed by whatever his reasoning skills were. He was good around my friends and usually got along very well, but there were moments when he wanted to test the situation.

Back then, Mike enjoyed drinking beer, sometimes in excess. This should have been a telltale sign for me, but once again, I had my blinders on tight and wasn't willing to see the situation for what it was. "What can a few beers do? Don't worry, everything will be all right," I told myself and everyone that confronted me about the situation, thinking that there was a problem.

When Mike was 18, his parents divorced. His father became homeless. I knew this haunted Mike, having quite an effect on him, as it would any young and still impressionable person. We didn't talk much about it, and like the beer that comes bottled up, so too, were Mike's thoughts and emotions.

I was just 21 and Mike was 23 when we married in front of about 120 guests on May 29, 1983, at the Itasca Country Club. I wore my mother's wedding dress and had five maids of honor with five groomsmen. It was a very traditional Lutheran wedding.

A few months after our wedding, we bought and moved into a repossessed, two-story house in Palatine. Looking forward, we were planning to have kids, or so I thought. After a year of marriage, I was pregnant for the first time, but miscarried. Three months later, I was pregnant again.

There were no complications and this time around everything went smoothly, though more quickly than planned. Baby Michael arrived on Jan 4th , one month early.

That afternoon, I had just come home with bags of groceries, and instead of carrying one bag at a time, I loaded down my hips with two. Mike, a gear-head, was in the garage with the door halfway down because he was painting a '64 Chevy Impala. I asked him if he could help me bring in the groceries, but he was too busy.

When I made my way under the garage door as though I were in a limbo contest, baby Michael's foot penetrated my water bag. Suddenly, I appeared to be peeing all over the garage floor. Mike got upset and asked me what I was doing. I had no answer. I was in panic.

Calling my mom, I found out what was happening. She told me to call the doctor and go to the hospital.

When I spoke to the doctor, he urged me to come right in. Trying to get Mike to stop working on his car was like trying to pull your own teeth; it just wasn't going to happen. Mike grew angry with me for being such an inconvenience, "Now the paint's not going to dry right!" He bitched and moaned, while grudgingly driving me to the hospital.

My parents met me at the hospital and the doctor

tried to get the Pitocin going so I could deliver naturally. After 30 hours of labor, I was given a C-section and son Michael was born — all seven pounds and 12 ounces of him.

Husband Mike didn't really know what to do and was never hands-on with the kids. When he held baby Michael, I often wondered what he was thinking. I didn't believe he truly appreciated the fact that he helped create another human being, a life. He rarely changed diapers and preferred being with his buddies, than to be with his family. Occasionally, he did play with the baby and it was a jaw-dropping anomaly. I truly just didn't expect it. It really was something I cherished seeing him do.

I wanted Mike to be like my father who walked through the door after a busy day and enjoyed being wrestled to the floor by kids hanging all over him. Mike's greeting wasn't anything close, "I've got some things to do. I'll be back later." And out the door he'd go, leaving me to cope after having worked a full day myself.

Since Mike was employed by my dad he had to show up, but sometimes he was declared to be missing in action. My father put up with this and even brought out one of Mike's strengths; a real talent for building things to exact precision. I'm not sure if dad ever told him, but he gave Mike work that needed to be done right the first time.

At home, Mike and I argued over his drinking. When I was nine months pregnant with Briana and holding five-month-old Michael, Mike came in ranting and raving about something. Finally, nudging passed me rather hard he ended up breaking a bedroom window. He left the house and I instantly called my parents and then the cops. For hours, I worried about where he was, knowing that he was drinking and hoping he was safe.

When it got really late and we figured Mike wasn't coming home, my father suggested we try to trace his gas card. With police help, we learned that Mike was headed toward Minnesota and I instantly knew where he was going. I called an old buddy of Mike's and warned him that Mike would probably be showing up soon. When he got to his friend's house, he was told to call home.

I was actually surprised when Mike called. I was even more surprised to hear, "I'm moving to Minnesota. I packed all my tools and I've left for good."

I said, "Mike, that's crazy. You belong here with your family, your kids. Our baby is due in a few weeks!"

A day or so later he was home again. There was no airing of his feelings; he was just as closed off as ever. Saying sorry was certainly never in his vocabulary. He went back to work. I wouldn't understand what was really happening within him until years later.

Though Mike never physically hurt me, he did punch in quite a few walls, broke a lot of glass and damaged valuables. Sometimes when we were arguing in the car, he'd start driving really fast to scare me. He railed against my family, how much they pissed him off, how they didn't like him. The blinders were coming off. I was truly seeing what my grandfather and my parents had warned me about. Then my beautiful daughter was born.

Briana was delivered by C-section. There were no long hours of labor. This time I knew what to expect. Again, Mike was not around when I needed him.

When my kids were little, I thought Briana had the best chance of melting her dad's heart. She reached out to Mike so often, her little hands up and asking to be held. It broke my heart to see my child rejected by her father. It was another billboard size of a sign that I was overlooking.

During this time, I was doing odd jobs like sewing, cutting hair and the payroll for my dad's business. Things just weren't clicking financially, so I looked for steady work.

In the early part of my marriage, but before my pregancies, my sister Lisa, Mary Ellen (sister-in-law) and I all found jobs through the newspaper and started work at Wick's Lumber Company on the very same day. As a buyer's assistant, I earned about $20K per year. Occupationally, things were looking up.

Shortly after I started work, Wick's hired a new lumber buyer, Donn Gunvalson, and I became his secretary. Rumor had it that Donn had moved from San Diego and was a confirmed bachelor.

Many of the ladies were hot for Donn and I was warned to stay out of their way. I tried to tell my friends, "Look, I'm married. I love Mike. I don't care about this new guy Donn."

Donn was a very good and ethical manager. He and I got along fine and it was obvious that there could be more, but I was married. We never kissed, hugged or crossed the line, though there were flirtatious innuendos.

I sometimes wondered if I was married to the wrong man. Admittedly, I kept Donn in the back of my mind, sort of like an ace in the hole. If Mike and I didn't work out, I thought Donn might like me enough to pursue a relationship. I tried to shake it off. Life went on and I had to rid myself of these thoughts. After another six months at Wick's Lumber, Donn was gone. He decided to leave for work in California and avoid the cold Mid-western winters.

Over the years, we kept in touch via letters. Eventually, I began to send pictures of new-born Michael and then Briana. Then the return letters stopped. Donn was considering marrying another woman and we lost all contact. I was five years into my marriage and trying to make the best of it.

In those days, Mike wasn't a man who could be depended on. Every time I thought I could rely on him, I was disappointed. I kept the more stable, dependable and responsible man, Donn, in my thoughts and wondered if there was a chance I'd someday live in sunny Southern California. Unfortunately, this hope waned since I was certain he had gotten married.

About eight and a half years into my marriage, I wrote in my diary about how un-happy I was with Mike. I just didn't know how I was going to make it through my life with this man. He was still drinking, not showing up for work, and from what I learned he wasn't being faithful.

Every January my parents and I, along with my kids, went to Puerto Vallarta where my folks had a condo. Mike, always welcome, never came along — not once. He missed many family functions and just didn't want to share what I thought was the good life.

One rainy night, I found myself standing on the balcony and staring out at the dark and rainy Banderas Bay. My father came out to be with me and asked if I wanted or needed to talk. I proceeded to explain how Mike just doesn't want this good life I'm trying to build. "We're like oil and water. I don't know how I'm going to make this work," I confided.

"Vicki," he said, "you know we don't condone divorce under any circumstances; but for this once, we understand that, if you don't leave Mike, the kids will suffer. We hate the idea of divorce and don't believe in it. However, in your case we encourage you to make critical changes in your life. We'll be here for you financially and emotionally, but you have to figure this out on your own. You will need to get a long-term plan in place to provide for yourself and your children, because Mike can't be counted on financially."

Here I was, 28 years old, always wanting to make my parents proud, never disappointed. Had they told me to stick it out, I would have. When I got home from the trip, I asked Mike if he wanted a divorce. Halfway hoping he would say no and want to fight for our relationship, I was somehow relieved when he said yes.

To make sure I was doing the right thing, I sought out pastoral guidance and was told there are three things that the church recognized as grounds for officially dissolving a marriage: the three As – Addiction, Adultery and Abuse. Mike was drinking alcohol, chasing skirts and verbally abusive beyond anything I wanted for myself or my kids for the rest of our lives.

He also managed to get a DUI while we were going through the divorce. He led police on a high-speed chase that ended with his being maced. He tried to blame me for his drunk-driving charge. First he had to drink because we were together. Now he drank because we were divorcing. That wasn't my problem. I had to move beyond Mike.

Soon, it was all over. My attorney in Palatine couldn't get the court processing my divorce paperwork fast enough to suit me. I was done. Six weeks later, on our ninth anniversary, May 29, 1992, we were officially over, caput, finished.

I wanted to be fair about everything so we split all of our assets down the middle. I was supposed to get $660 a month in child support. He was still working for my father, so he'd get three checks per month and I'd get his fourth, which was 25% of his salary. That lasted about a year. Mike quit working for my dad and I never received much support from that point on. Occasionally, he gave me some baby-sitter money. Mostly, my mother looked after the kids while I worked and Mike did nothing.

Together, we owned our home and a rental unit. We lived in the house until it sold. From there, Mike moved to the rental unit, which he got in the divorce, while I took my money from the house sale and purchased my own condo. Unfortunately, Mike managed to lose the rental property. He just quit making the mortgage payments.

Immediately following the divorce, I was scared. I wanted to make sure I was able to raise two kids alone. I wasn't exactly sure how I was going to support them. The kids and I moved to the small condo and I somehow managed to make ends meet.

There were some nights that I had to call the cops because Mike was still trying to insinuate himself back in my life — sleeping in my driveway, trying to crawl through windows.

Now, when I ask myself how I hooked up with such a man, I realize that I can only blame myself. I sometimes think that, if I had gone away to college, I wouldn't have jumped into marriage. I definitely wanted some kind of validation that I wasn't a loser and I was doing something with my life. I visualized myself being a young mom, staying at home and having babies — living the lifestyle of my parents. In my mind, I created this world where my sense of purpose would come from marrying Mike. I'd get started with my life and not be stuck in limbo. I made a choice and had two wonderful children to show for it. I also knew a lot more about myself and what I wanted out of life.

I started selling life insurance right away after the divorce. While married, I had bought a life insurance policy on Mike, in case he'd gotten killed while driving under the influence. The insurance person was a friend, who told me how much she made off my one policy — $600. I was floored. I thought I could easily do this. She told me how to get my license and I never looked back. In an industry dominated by men, we were the only two women employed by this particular office of Western Southern Life Insurance. She and I competed against one another and outsold everyone else in the office.

About a week before my divorce was final, I was out at a nice restaurant having a glass of wine with a friend and in walked Donn Gunvalson. After not seeing him for nine years, I had to get a closer look. Walking up to him, I instantly recognized the stance and mannerisms of the man I'd once known and admired.

What followed was a lightning round of catching up. I had a million questions: Was he married? Did he have a girlfriend? Did he have kids? I got around to asking them all and he responded without hesitation. I was really impressed that he was able to handle my aggressive inquisition. He was what I consider a real man.

In turn, Donn asked if I was ever going to get rid of that husband of mine. What a perfectly timed question. Meeting Donn again after all those years was more than luck; it was divine intervention. I proceeded to tell him that my divorce would be final next week. He smiled, handed me his new business card and relayed the news that he was back in Chicago.

I've never believed in the three-day rule for calling someone, especially when that someone is a person you really like and respected. I wondered if I willed Donn to reappear in my life. POOF! He's back. Yes, the universe does work in mysterious ways.

I started dating Donn, though at times I felt very insecure. I couldn't help but wonder why this man would want to get involved with a divorcee and two kids. I came up with reasons why he shouldn't pursue me; he's older, more established, he could date anyone. Why me?

Donn was very reassuring when he'd say that actions speak louder than words. When he said, "I wouldn't be with you if I didn't want to be," I believed him. He said he liked me because I was independent, not needy.

My parents were elated when they met Donn. They really liked that he was smart, older, established, a good business man. Donn and my dad got along really well and truly respected one another. He made it very clear to my folks that he was going to take care of me and the kids. He made big promises and always came through. He was a real grown-up, and again, a real man.

It was unfortunate that the kids had been hurt so badly by Mike that they kept Donn at a distance. Even today, I feel they could be closer except for the damage previously done by their father.

I was busy working nights in the insurance industry, and Donn stepped in and watched the kids for me. Here was this 42-year-old, confirmed bachelor, caring for my kids the way their father never did. I was amazed at his ability in tackling a ready-made family and becoming such a caring member.

Though Donn and I didn't live together before marriage, we did become a blended family. For better or worse, I kept the role of the disciplinarian when it came to the kids, and I think this sometimes angered Donn. I wouldn't let him make any decisions about their actions. My justification was that these were my kids, and if he could decide to leave, they were to know that I wasn't going anywhere. They would answer to me, the one with THE look. Hmmm, just like my dad — the apple never falls far from the tree.

While I was busy selling insurance, I was also still working for my dad doing payroll on the side — anything to make more money. There came a point where my dad started to go through a serious battle with his memory. It was painful to watch. He would inform everyone in the office that he was going to a job site for an estimate, but hours later, the potential client would call and ask where he was.

My dad would eventually return to the office and I'd ask him where he'd been. He'd tell me he went to bid a job and when confronted with the facts, he grew flustered and angry. "I told you I went there to do an estimate!" He would charge.

That was the beginning of the end for my father. After we found him wandering down the side of the road one day, it was obvious he was lost. When we asked him what he was doing, he couldn't respond. He couldn't remember who he was.

At the age of 59, my dad was diagnosed with Alzheimer's, but refused to believe that he wasn't going to get better, "We'll get through this. We'll cure this. I'll be fine." However, the doctor was very blunt with my dad and informed him that there was no cure. And so little by little, my dad was relieved of his responsibilities.

It was difficult watching this man who was a type-A personality, stripped of his greatness. He had such command of so many things, but was slowly losing the ability to perform the simplest tasks without supervision.

Eventually, Billy completely took over the business, and years later, my father had to be put in a nursing home for his own safety. He battled Alzheimer's for almost nine years before his passing at the age of 67. I was so happy he had gotten to know Donn before losing his faculties. And he was still around to see the two of us get married.

Donn and I would marry in front of 120 guests at a clubhouse in Barrington. Michael and Briana walked me down the aisle and were the best man and maid of honor. It was just the four of us, nothing too extravagant, but very nice just the same.

Two weeks before marrying Donn, I knew that I would soon be leaving Chicago. He had accepted a job in California. Suddenly, it seemed another one of my fantasies was about to come true. I had always liked the idea of living in Southern California. Though I would lose all of my residual income when I left Western Southern Life Insurance, I was now going to be a mom and housewife and live the good life.

I put my condo up for sale and in the coming months, Donn and I visited Southern California to find the perfect house. During this time, I went back to court to prove that Mike was an unfit father, who wasn't providing for his kids, had rarely seen them and offered absolutely no support. The court granted me sole custody and the right to take my kids and move out of the state.

Donn and I finally settled into our new home in Mission Viejo. I just knew I'd reached a new pinnacle in my life. I was happily married to a stable man and we seemed to work through any rough spots in our relationship until our first real argument.

I grew up watching and learning from my father, who taught us to go out and work for what we wanted. Though Donn was going to be the breadwinner in our family, I came to realize that there were some differences to work out.

The first argument we had was about money. Donn and I had blended our finances when we bought the house, but there was little discussion about control or spending.

New to California, I was told about Costco, a discount bulk warehouse not found in Chicago. Loading the kids in the family mini-van, we headed to Costco on a shopping spree to load up on things I felt we needed.

Donn and I had about $800 in our account and I knew he was getting paid at the end of the week, so I spent $400 without worrying. I packed the van full of things like food, snacks, beverages, pool toys, clothes and quite a few other items.

Back home, I backed the van up to the garage and told the kids to go inside. When Donn came out and saw what I was unloading, he got angry. I quickly tried to make him understand that I'd found this great place to buy everything we needed in bulk and blah, blah, blah. He let me know in his terms that money couldn't be spent like this.

I instantly felt empty, like a small, chided child. I didn't know what to do. I called my parents and told them I might have made a horrible mistake. My father calmed me down and said, "Vicki, you made the absolute right choice in marrying Donn, but you must realize he's been a bachelor all these years. He's never shopped like this and you can't expect him to understand. You just need to work things out and communicate better."

My father's last suggestion was to bite my lip and appreciate learning new things about relationships. Then he suggested the possibility of my returning to work so I could remain independent and feel freer about spending.

It was then and there that I made a personal goal to do better than Donn when it came to making money. This wasn't to emasculate him or show him up; it was to prove something to myself. I liked what money could buy for me and the kids with or without Donn, so I would make my own and direct my own life, even while married.

I went right out and signed up for a class to get my insurance license. After 52 hours of lectures and study, I took my test and passed. From that point on, I was a licensed California insurance agent.

My first year in sales I didn't beat Donn's income, but that was okay. I was making my own money. We had joint accounts. I felt good about contributing to the family income and I could buy things without having to ask permission.

By my third year in life insurance sales, I hit my goal. I passed Donn's income. I wondered if Donn fully realized the type of woman he had married. I hoped he would appreciate my capabilities and not feel threatened. And that's the way it worked out. He's still the strong, stable man I married, and money isn't a factor when it comes to how we treat each other. I completely respect his ability to maintain an incredible work ethic for a corporation which requires a lot from him and I know he respects my ability to create a profitable and sustainable business.

I have my father to thank for so much. He taught me that life could be unpredictable, but hard work, tenacity and confidence could see me through hard times. I grew up, married the wrong man, divorced, married the right man, brought two beautiful children into the world and started my own successful business. I made the choices that got me where I am. Some were better than others, but I kept working at a better life.

MORE THAN A HOUSEWIFE

Chapter Three

Purpose and Direction

Growth of Self

How fortunate I am! There are millions of people in the world who have tried and failed over and over again. We learn from our failures and we grow with our successes. I think it's important to occasionally stop and appreciate how far I've come, the significance of the journey.

Though I was raised in a good home, I experienced my share of rough roads. I occasionally like to think of those roads as being extremely muddy. With each step I take, my foot sinks deep. Each time I pull a foot up to take my next step the suction damn near pulls the shoe right off.

The great thing about traveling those muddy roads is that when I made it to dry ground, and I looked back at the deep and empty impressions, I realized that I'd made it out; I looked at my past, I acknowledge the courage, and I set my sights toward a better future. There will most certainly be more muddy roads, but I know how to slog through. I may falter, but I won't lose my balance. I will not fall.

Some people never think about keeping their balance or about their next step; maintaining solid footing with their relationships, careers or finances. I know there was a time when I didn't. I used to flounder quite a bit. I didn't know what my purpose was and definitely didn't have a direction. Growing and realizing one's potential requires both.

Without these two ingredients of life, purpose and direction, the world around us is hard to navigate. Do you go through each day doing the same exact thing you did yesterday? Wake up, go to work, eat lunch, drive home, take care of domestic things and go back to sleep. If you're happy with your day-to-day life, I think it's because you have a purpose, that there is a reason you do what you do.

Each day I get up and know exactly what my day will be like. Bits and pieces of it may change here and there, but for the most part, I'm going to be serving others — that's my purpose. Some may think I'm a workaholic, but when you love and get gratification all day long from what you're doing, then being a workaholic is not an addiction; it's a calling.

The first sentence of the last paragraph, talked about what my day will be like. I said this intentionally. It's not, what my day will bring. I believe I make my day through design: setting goals, staying focused and getting things done. Occasionally, I incur a few unsubscribed intrusions during the day, add them to my to-do list and cross them off when resolved.

When I graduated high school, I had no known talent, purpose or direction. I wasn't college material and though I got a cosmetology certificate, I knew it wasn't going to give me the lifestyle I desired. I'd seen my parents make a wonderful life for their kids and I wanted to do the same thing for my children. Unfortunately, I got stuck in the mud for a while.

One of the things I took with me from beauty college was discipline. Since I knew I wasn't getting a university degree, I had to have something that said I could set a goal and achieve it. After 1500 hours of class time, I prevailed when others dropped out. I was proud of myself for completing the requirements and getting my certificate.

That one single part of my life (hair styling), though not used in any way other than personal care, taught me that I could challenge and discipline myself to create whatever I really wanted. Along with my father teaching through example, I now understood that I also had a good work ethic and found that discipline is the way through the mud.

What is your real purpose in life? How does one find it? Since you were a young kid you've had an affinity for something. As an example: I liked making sure friends were happy and having a good time. I didn't know this would end up being a part of my real purpose. I wasn't born with this affinity for others. Having ethics or discipline didn't help me find my passion.

Within you at this moment, your purpose waits to be recognized. You have a specific passion or desire to help in some way. Once you're aware of it, suddenly the curtains open and the world becomes your stage. When I examine what a purpose is not, it helps me to define exactly why I'm doing what I do.

We've all heard how little Joey grew up with a baseball in his hand. He was so good that he would one day be a professional player. He could track a grounder, throw at lightning speed and see the bat hit the ball every time. This is a talent, not a purpose. Joey has a very high awareness level regarding his ability to play ball. Everyone that is good at what they do, their talent, it's because of their awareness level on that particular ability.

Shellie has always had an ability to instantly resolve accounting problems. You might hear someone say that she was born to do that. Again, it's a talent, not a purpose. Shellie is very aware of what she does. Anyone can be good at accounting if they apply themselves.

Talent or ability is an awareness level and a purpose is a service. Joey is talented in baseball and makes a lot of money which he uses to serve his favorite charity. Shellie does financially well as an accountant and uses her talent to tutor kids in math, which brings her joy.

A writer informs, a doctor heals, a tutor reveals, an artist creates wonder in the minds, a scientist searches for answers to help mankind. Each occupation not only creates a living for someone, but also services humanity in some fashion. Find your talent, and your purpose won't be far away.

I rarely ever confronted the need for a purpose while growing up. I went with the flow. Through my youth, I enjoyed showing friends a good time at our cabin on the lake — sharing waterskiing and snowmobiling experiences with others. I tried to get Mike to appreciate the good things in life that he had missed out on. I wanted others to have an opportunity to share in the happiness and carefree moments. I didn't realize I was fulfilling my purpose.

My parents' purpose to give their kids a better life may have become part of my purpose. I may have married Mike to understand what was worth having and what was not, what a good life consists of, and what a mirage is. Through insurance, I get to help others protect what they have, to maintain the good life, to plan for their families. I watched as my father's business took a sudden and horrific turn, and later his mind betrayed him. I wanted to take some of the risk out of life. Insurance did that.

When I divorced, I needed work that would enable me to provide for myself and the kids. I remembered distant family members working in the insurance industry and doing very well. My friend Laura, a divorced mother of three, who had sold a policy to me on Mike, was doing financially well. It was Laura who helped me with the process of getting licensed. I would complete a class requirement of 52 hours to qualify for the state exam. Within weeks I had my license to sell life insurance. At this point I didn't know I was moving into alignment with my purpose.

I previously explained that Donn was my impetus for getting into the insurance industry the second time around — I didn't want to be told how I could spend money. This was the beginning of a new growth stage for me.

Since I wasn't born with this purpose and I rarely questioned if I had one, some might say that I fell into it.

Sometimes that happens. If you're particularly happy with what you do, I'd say you're in the right field for your talent. If you don't like your occupation, I suggest a conference with your past.

Think back. Did your English teachers look forward to your short stories? Were you an artist with a palette and brush? Perhaps, you were really into TV shows about cooking and you should be a master chef. Maybe you were into crafting things with clay, wood or medal. When talent and purpose are recognized, then one needs to carefully bond them together.

In my early adult life, I was just going through the motions, kind of like putting a plate on the table or tying one's shoes. I worked jobs for paychecks and the office interaction. I felt normal being in a group of people who punched a clock and basically shared the same lifestyle as me. It was almost like a continuation of high school. The unfortunate part, in some respect, was that I was kind of letting myself down. I might not have been the best student in the world, but I could be focused when I wanted something. I just didn't know what that something was. I was in limbo trying to find a reason to expect more of myself.

When I started working at Wick's I didn't have a college degree and was paid less. There were a few women in my department who did have degrees, and though I sometimes felt inferior to them, I still knew I was valuable to the company. You will always be as valuable as you want yourself to be. Even without a degree, I was a quick study and did good work. But I didn't have real direction. It took a while. Now, I always look for ways to expand my skills and take on more responsibility to be worth more, to earn more.

Once you know your talent or purpose, you still have to overcome negativity: "You can't do that!" "You need a degree for that!" "You can't just start over." Don't be discouraged. But if there is something you should be doing with your life, do it. Get the proper education if it's needed. A death row attorney won't make much money, but if they save one life by proving innocence, their purpose is served. They got the proper education that enabled them to serve their purpose — saving a life.

Finding our talent and purpose can help to re-direct us into becoming pilots, doctors, senators, fire-fighters, entertainers or any other field. The serious study, training and dedication give direction to become who we choose to be and how we choose to serve.

For a while, I thought that going to school, getting married to Mike, and having kids was my purpose, but I still felt unfulfilled. Something was seriously missing. Motherhood certainly made me feel that I was here for a reason, but it wasn't until I found my calling in helping others that I found my true purpose. At first, I thought the money was the main draw, but I realized that the real satisfaction from helping people safeguard their families and being there when they needed me was exactly what I needed and wanted.

When a client passes away, and I present a check to the spouse, reassuring them they're financially safe, I get instant gratification. I'm doing what I absolutely love. When a mother of three receives a check that will help her to continue paying the mortgage, put her kids through college, and allow her to breathe, I've not only done my job, I've served a greatest and most meaningful purpose.

Wick's Lumber was a good training ground for my adult life. I was held accountable for my work and learned to take orders. I had to hold onto this job because I was a married adult. If fired I couldn't go running home to my parents.

Being 22 and having a mortgage was not the norm in the early 80s, but I was driven. I knew I wanted nice things and I was determined to get them. My mother always had great taste in home décor and I wanted this kind of lifestyle. Handling payroll for my father taught me how to pay my bills and budget for the things I needed or wanted. I was able to gain the tokens of success: a nice house with an inviting ambiance, a deck in the back with a fenced-in yard and a dog. We were living like other couples, only we were younger and getting a head-start. Still, I always wanted more and knew I was capable of getting it.

While married to Mike, we bought a rental house, which increased our worth. I wanted him to drive a good car and have nice things. None of this seemed to matter to him, but it mattered to me. Success mattered to me. I wanted to be able to measure how far I'd come by how I lived. Again, I knew what I wanted and where I had to go to get it.

I saw my career in insurance as the ends to meet my goals. During the week, the sales numbers would be posted next to the agent's name. I'd hold off turning in my numbers. I didn't want anyone to know where they stood against me during the week, until the last minute. It was a dog-eat-dog world and I was determined to be the big dog.

The real competition came from my friend Laura. She and I played this game between ourselves, but mostly against the unsuspecting males who dominated the office. After only two months in the business, Laura and I bought brand new cars; hers was an Infinity and mine was a Lexus. When we pulled up to the office and parked side by side, our boss Mark glared at us and scoffed, "What are you thinking? You can't afford those cars!" Laura and I looked at each other and smiled at our boss. We were enjoying our success.

Never let anyone tell you that you can't do something. If they do, create a plan to prove them 100% wrong. Get a purpose! Set a direction! Take action!

Friendly competition has got to be one of the best motivators for creating success. Whether you're trying to lose weight, increase sales or win a big game, find a friend.

If you truly want to make a difference in your life, you're the one that has to do it, not your parents, siblings, friends, spouse. You have to believe in yourself. "This is my life and I control it; I own it!"

I realized that I'm a competitor. Even if I didn't have someone to compete against, I competed against myself. You might ask, "How can you compete against yourself?" Look at your own highest sales, your best times, your most wins and do more. Look at yourself in the mirror and introduce yourself to your competition. Go beyond what you've ever done before.

Once you do find a purpose to serve, you'll never doubt it. You won't ever dream of doing anything else. You'll feel content, able to breathe easier. You'll never look back and wonder if you made the right move. You'll just know.

Don't let others hold you back. Surround yourself with like-minded individuals who give of themselves. When you encounter negative people in your life, move on, find positive influences. The only person you can change is yourself. Just realize that the more you try to change, the more others may want to knock you down. Too often your success reflects their failure. Use what encouragement you can get and throw away the naysaying.

In addition to monetary rewards and personal satisfaction, my job in the insurance industry gave me flexibility with my schedule. I was a single mom with two kids and needed this flexibility for attending their special events. I owe a special thanks to my brother, Billy, my parents, Lisa and Donn for taking care of my kids in the evenings when I had to meet with a client. No matter how independent you think you are, you always need family and friends. They help you all along the way and should be appreciated for their contribution to your success.

If you happen to be a single parent and need work that is flexible, look for work that matches your needs and that can also help fulfill your purpose.

Though I'd never want children to suffer, I've seen too many single mothers give up profitable careers because they believed their kids would be hurt, be deprived of attention. I know how hard it is to leave for work when a child is crying, "Mommy, Mommy, don't go." I was sometimes over-whelmed with guilt, saying goodbye to those sweet faces. It was heart-wrenching. But I felt I was being a good parent by providing for my children, giving them a home, making sure they ate well and had proper clothing.

I had to do a lot of growing up to get where I am today. Nothing has been handed to me. I never expected anything from anyone that I wasn't willing to work for. When I received kindness, I was most appreciative. I learned long ago that accepting good things from others is just as important as giving of yourself. It's good to let people do things for you sometimes. It makes them feel good and validates your own worth. It's part of the give and take of life.

This positive flow, has direction and effect. It feels good to contribute, to give back, to provide others a chance to add something to your life.

Life is indeed an incredible journey. Even the muddy roads take you places. And there is opportunity around every corner. "Ask and you shall receive," is how the Bible puts it. Just make sure to ask the right questions that help you find your purpose and then direct your future with the answers you receive.

Many people can become successful and yet not serve an intentional purpose for others. A man becomes an airline pilot and transports people from coast to coast. His real intention is to be amongst the clouds. His purpose is self-serving and though he may be a talented pilot, until he recognizes the value of the lives he's been entrusted with, he's just pushing tin.

It's okay for people to have self-serving purposes, but one day they will become bored due to a lack of creativity. Human beings that don't continue to create will easily become burned-out with what they once desired. This happens in one's personal life as well as business. When you create or serve others it keeps the heart alive with verve.

How does one create direction? Sure, we know where

we have to go when we want a cookie … directly to the cookie jar, but when we want to create a bigger and better lifestyle, what does direction really mean?

Direction means planning. A movie director plans each scene he will shoot. He envisions exactly what it will look like from the beginning and what he expects the results to be in the end. He knows every single scene he will shoot between the first, "Roll 'em," to the last … "That's a wrap!"

Picture yourself as a talented director and plan exactly how your business or your life is going to play out, scene by scene. Your purpose is to have an eventual effect on your audience, your clients. Like the director of a film, people are coming to see you because they know you're going to serve them what they desire. Whereas a film director serves up passion, fear, mystery or makes people laugh through comedy, your audience may come to you for safety, inspiration, education or any myriad of purposes that serve them.

Talent plus Purpose with Direction leads to a successful life that can't be ignored. In the end, if you followed your direction (plans) correctly, perhaps slightly adjusting along the way, you'll find that your directions will have helped you serve your purpose well.

Purpose is the key to your future, but won't move an inch or get you to where you want to be, without direction. Then again, action/drive is the third ingredient, and without it, purpose and direction are just pretty thoughts.

Chapter Four

Driven

In the Blood

It's all about the Little-Red-Hen syndrome – the story about the hen that went around the farm and asked all the other animals to help put ingredients together to make bread. No one wanted to help make the bread, but everyone wanted to take part in eating it.

When you look at who the most financially successful people are, you'll find they aren't trust-fund babies, but they are little red hens. They are the people who plan, organize and make things happen.

I shake my head when I hear people complain about the wealthy in our society. They speak out in negativity because they lack the ability to reach for their desires beyond their acceptance level. To be annoyed by someone's wealth is senseless. I think the naysayers may have wealth confused with arrogance.

Yes, there are corporations run by wealthy people who believe they can do whatever they wish, but this set of wealthy are not the majority. Because of the sole proprietors that have created wealth for themselves through business, there are jobs available that feed families. Like the red hen, those who take the risk, create the bread.

Criticizing the wealthy while purchasing lottery tickets and hoping to become rich is like the farm animals; they want the greatest return for the least amount of effort.

55

I often wonder how much the complainers could accomplish if they took all that negative energy and used it as a source for creating a better life. I tend to believe that pinning all of your hopes on winning the lottery says you don't have faith in your own ability. I'm not knocking the lottery system, because even wealthy people play it, but to put faith in something with less than million-to-one odds is just ridiculous.

Driven people don't put much faith in freebies and certainly don't wait around for someone else to fulfill their desires. They plan a strategy, and propel themselves forward with sheer will.

I can't honestly say that I've been driven throughout my whole life. As a matter of fact, it's almost impossible to do. If one is always in the driven mode, they'll eventually break down through exhaustion. When you know your purpose, and you make your plans or your direction, then action is where being driven gets implemented.

While growing up, I was fortunate to see how driven my father was. He never lectured us kids, but taught by example. The beautiful home, the trips to the lake house or the cross-country travel was all inclusive of a man with desires, direction and drive.

The last chapter talked about purpose and direction and their importance to being successful. The many ways there are for success are easily matched by the number of ways to fail. Knowing what you should not do is just as important to success as knowing what should be done. How well you follow a strategy will be one of the determining factors to your success.

To make clear, when I talk about being successful, I'm not always talking about monetary gains. I'm talking about having positive results with the desires that consume the mind daily. Do you want to lose weight? Do you want to learn a certain subject? How can I better my situation?

A strategy is a plan for achieving a favorable end result. If I told you that it was important to make a to-do list each day, but as equally important to make a to-don't list, would you laugh?

If on your to-do list you noted that you want to lose weight, then your to-don't list should have something that helps you with that — don't drink soda, don't eat fast food, don't eat late in the evening. Having a to-do list is great, but not having to-don't lists is a major factor in the parlay of what you truly desire.

Driven people often attack life from both sides. Like the do/don't lists that compliment each other, a driven person knows that just wanting something to happen, without understanding how things happen, is contradictory to success.

What should someone do when they realize they've never been driven in any area of their life? Maybe they've followed the crowd for as long as they can remember, but now they realize they need to break free from the pack. Well, the first thing I will tell you is that it won't be easy. Then second is — it will only be as hard as you make it.

People set up patterns throughout their lives. They get comfortable with what they've sometimes subconsciously created and can feel strange about stepping out of what now feels normal. Have you ever seen any makeover shows on TV? They take an average person that doesn't have any real sense of style and after a little work through presentation and coaching, the person comes out with a new hairstyle and clothing that accents certain aspects and forms.

Usually, the person is elated in their newfound change. The sad thing is that often, because of patterns, the person goes home and eventually changes everything back. If this were you, I would suggest you unbury those clothes and reintroduce your friends to the new, improved you.

One is fortunate when they become aware of what they feel inadequate about. It's the one chance available to understand that their past is holding them back from success in the inadequate area. What is unfortunate is that most people won't give a second glance at these relevant yet uneasy thoughts. Taking the time to process your thoughts is the key to making necessary changes to patterns in your life

As an example, women are especially susceptible to hating a new hairstyle when they first step in front of their friends. They know that others are going to have an opinion. This can lead to hurt feelings if those opinions don't match their own. Hmmm, so what does this have to do with being driven? Well, driven people tend to not care what others think about them. They're going to make changes and find what works.

In this hairstyle example, let me ask you this: If you changed your hairstyle and your friends didn't like it, but then you went on a business call to an office and some person you were meeting for the first time commented on how nice your hair is, what would you do? Hopefully, you would thank them for the compliment and let them believe that this is your regular style.

Oftentimes, friends who know you in one way become uncomfortable when you change. Change can literally seem like a threat to those who don't dream of a better future.

Being driven isn't always in the blood. My father was driven, but I wasn't for quite some time. I had to change the way I thought about my life. I had to understand what it would mean to me if I were to have direction and drive. I had to change my patterns and accept that I was as capable of success and wealth as people hundreds of times more successful and wealthier.

There were lessons I didn't want to learn because I thought I was doing fine, but eventually I had to swallow my pride and admit that perhaps I wasn't as efficient as I could be.

Look around your life and analyze your situation right now. Are you a single mother with kids of a deadbeat dad? Do you have a husband that won't help out around the house, or one that is loafing on your couch while you try to make financial ends meet? What is going on around you? I hope for your sake you're surrounding yourself with positive people that have clear-cut goals.

I find that many people that are driven work at remaining busy all day long. They're striking lines through their to-do list and making life happen. How many items on your list did you cross out today? Did you make a list?

When you analyze where you are in life, you start the process of organization. You can instantly expect chaos to show up when you begin to care about your path, your direction. A spouse or friend may chuckle and say, 'What makes you think you can do that?" Understand that when this happens you need to listen to them and know that their critical thought is really about their own inability to believe in themselves, so they have to deflect it upon you.

My friends from WOW (Women of Wisdom, Women of Wealth) have husbands that believe in them and encourage them to influence or empower women across the nation. These men don't feel the least bit threatened by a woman with drive. I would dare to say that these men appreciate power, regardless from whom it's being delivered. What I'm getting at is this — if your spouse puts down your dreams, then they're not worthy of you, they're afraid and lack faith in their ability, not yours.

Create in your mind, first, the drive you desire to have and it will eventually become a part of who you are. Friends and family will stand up and take notice. They'll have to because when you start moving a million miles and hour, they will have to try and dodge you or beg for you to not mow them over.

When you develop an incredible amount of drive toward your goals, you'll have to find communication time with the ones you love. People living in the driven mode 24/7 will inevitably break down and through the absence of balance, families can and will break apart. Life will always demand balance and you'll know, in one chaotic form or another, when things aren't right.

I'm a firm believer that women should never sit at

home and expect a man to provide for them. I do suggest, if you're putting all your eggs in one basket, you had better have an incredibly great plan in the case that basket fails. We've seen what the economy can do to families ill prepared.

Women shouldn't go back to work full time, if they have kids at home and a husband that provides well. What I'm saying is to find work that keeps your business acumen flowing in a positive direction and also creates income, at the least, for emergencies.

You may want to find a home-based business that offers flexibility during certain hours of the day. This way it would allow you to be home when the kids get out of school. As you probably know, I'm in the life insurance industry. It serves my purpose, but in the beginning it also allowed me flexibility in my day.

With every upside there is a downside. I've heard many horror stories regarding families not covered and the main income provider dies unexpectedly. Now, you may ask, what does this have to do with being driven?

Having handed out many checks to bereaved policy holders, I provide comfort when they know everything is going to be all right with their finances. I think it's sad, but I've never seen a woman become more driven than when her husband suddenly passes away. She now has to figure out how to provide for her family. Having a flexible business in place provides for emergencies, life or death.

Being driven is a state of mind and nothing more. One can be driven in any area they choose, mine happens to be business and making sure people are protected should the unthinkable happen.

As I titled this first section "Transitions," everything you've read thus far has been about making change. If your life is unbalanced in any way — an abusive marriage, an underpaying job, a heavy financial debt load, negative people surrounding you or a multitude of other life-draining experiences — I urge you to reconsider how you're handling

60

things and place an order in your mind for change because that's the only place a transition can start.

If you happen to be in one of the positions just mentioned, you must recognize it for what it is and speak about it openly. It is only then that you can begin to transition out of your situation.

I personally had to have enough drive to leave a marriage that I felt was bringing me down. I had to have the drive to get out into the real world and create work that supported my children and me. Everything I've experienceed, starting with my first operation when a child, to the failed marriage, has all been a part of my transitioning. So, you might ask, what am I transitioning to?

Eventually, I will get to a point where I'll relax and walk on the beach. I won't have a concern about time or the next meeting. My purpose is being fulfilled every day, but also as important, I'm going in the right direction of where I want to finish when I retire.

Right now, I'm strong minded with enough drive to get through the 12- to 15-hour days. I know this work will provide my family a very comfortable lifestyle upon my retirement. I believe people need to keep in mind that they will reach the end of the road where they can no longer work. If they're not prepared by any other means than Social Security, then I dare to claim they aren't thinking about their future survival, and whether they like it or not, there will come a day that they will struggle.

I believe it's a crime that children aren't taught from early adolescence exactly how our economy really works (behind the scenes) and how to be responsible with money. The all-mighty dollar is such an integral part of living, that to ignore its effect on one's future and not be driven to make as much as possible, is at times self-defeating. If you feel that it's greedy to be wealthy, it's probably because you were taught that money can't buy happiness. Well, you're 100% right. It won't buy happiness, but it can buy you some comfort throughout your life, while young and old. Don't be greedy, be smart and plan well.

If your vision is strong and you want change to happen in your life, then it will. But, before you go off and declare to all of your friends that everything is about to change dramatically, for the better, make sure your vision is precise. As an example: "I'd like a job that pays me $100K per year and I don't have to do a whole lot." Sorry to be the bearer of bad news, but that's just not reality. You'd be better off to know your talents and make your vision applicable to the desire. As an example…"I will offer my talent as a pastry chef. I will make specialty cakes for specific events such as weddings, corporate events, fine dining restaurants and other retail outlets that I attain through event planners and advertising."

I could go in depth on planning for the last example, but what I'm trying to get at is this: you need to be very specific about what you want and how you plan to get it.

I'm sure you've heard this before and it's something I always do: write out your goals and read them many times throughout your day. As you drill your desires into your mind, it changes the way you think and act. I know through experience that the more I think about what I want, and the direction I must take, the quicker things appear in the physical realm.

Let me take you back for a moment and show you that there was a time when you were extremely driven. Okay, maybe not extremely, but just the same, you had drive. When you were in elementary school and the bell began ringing after lunch, who was the first to get in line? Was it you? Did you race everyone and try to secure the number one position through the classroom door? Let me ask you this, did you eat your lunch as quickly as possible because you knew that being the first one on the playground meant that you were first at the handball court or other form of play?

Maybe you weren't into playground games, but in the classroom your hand always shot up to answer a tough question and prove that you knew your subject. Technically, yes, this is drive.

We all want to be the best at something. That will always be a deep-seated desire within us. Sometimes, over years of living a sedentary life, it's difficult to recall our desires, but more so, easier to negate them as folly, once remembered.

I want you to do this one little test to prove to yourself that you still have drive. This is an extremely easy way to understand the very basic meaning of drive. Find the nearest chair and decide to sit down for one minute. If you're already seated, then get up and move to another chair.

I hope you actually made the move. Now, believe it or not, that's drive at its most basic. You made a decision to do something and went forward with it. Yes, I know this was silly and simple, but it is just a small and easy way to inform you that your drive is always based on decision.

Do you want to create more drive? Don't fly from the seat of your pants, but plan your next move forward in life. Truth be known, everything you do is planned. You can't help but to plan. You did it when you went from standing to sitting. You did it when you crossed the room to a different chair. Plans don't have to be long and drawn out, but they should be given careful consideration if they're anything of real importance, like changing your life.

It's imperative that when you decide to have drive toward a known goal, family and friends around you get the memo. It doesn't matter what they do with the memo, but it is important that you adhere to what you say you're going to do.

When I decided that I was going to make my own money and spend it the way I wanted, I didn't necessarily tell Donn right away. I made actual plans about going back to work and then I created an opportunity to share my plans with Donn. He knew I wanted more than we collectively had the money for. Though he may have wanted a stay-at-home wife, I'm sure he enjoys the lifestyle the added money has produced: a beautiful home and many fun adventures.

What will make you get up and go? Who's your adversary? What's your impetus? Can you start today to be driven in your life? I truly hope you will. If the thought of taking action is difficult, write out a plan, take baby steps, just do it. I guarantee you won't regret it.

Speaking of regrets, those that are most memorable usually come at the end of a life. You know the one so many have said, "I wish I had done this or that."

I used to actually regret many things in my life. When I began to understand that regrets are strength and character building tools, I shifted my thoughts. I now realize that regret is just an un-happy way we handled something. We try to not regret too many things in our lives. In this way, we learn to not do certain things over and over. I'm now driven by those past mistakes or regrets and no longer bow my head in shame. I own them!

At this point, I'd like to add one more thing about me that some may not know. As you may recall, I admitted that I was lost after high school. I had no real talent, I didn't recognize my purpose and so there was no direction or drive. Though I changed my life by sticking to hard made decisions, it's incredible to me that in this great country of ours, millions of people are living this very moment without hope for a better future.

So many kids today are either dropping out of high school or barely graduating. Many kids haven't been taught to dream of bigger and better things or to be driven towards excellence. They might have seen their parents or friends just barely make ends meet and think — that's the way it's supposed to be.

Perhaps, if these kids had a realization of their past personal drive and achievements, and could draw enlightenment from them, they might once again reach down deep and reclaim what is there God-given right, success.

I didn't know my father was setting an example for us kids as we were growing, but I'm very aware that I have been setting an example for mine. When I work long hours and the kids see the fruit of my labor, they understand what it takes to create an affluent type of lifestyle. Later, if they so choose, it won't be such a mystery that applying drive produces results.

I'm not saying that this works 100% of the time, but I've seen many kids from humble backgrounds and hard-working parents, strive for great things.

As parents, we will always be setting an example, whether we believe we are or not? What are you sublimi-nally teaching your kids?

Section Two

Professionalism

MORE THAN A HOUSEWIFE

Chapter Five

Beginning in Business

The Growing Years

My first taste of business was sugary sweet. I was a little girl with my own Kool-Aid stand. My biggest customer was my father, and, boy, did he get the short end of the stick. He paid for the ingredients, I made the product, and he had to buy it — without a family discount.

As I got older and after receiving the certificate from beauty school, I thought I could make a business out of cutting hair. It turned out that I didn't like this line of work and definitely wouldn't make a living at it.

My next venture was sewing. I did many odd jobs, of which clothing was a small segment. Once, I made a set of valences for the kitchen of my neighbor. The woman had gotten an estimate of $4000 from a professional company and I low-balled them, cutting the price in half. Two grand in one week, I was ecstatic.

Though it seemed like I had sewed for an eternity that week, I liked the ability to make money while being at home with my kids. It was a win-win situation. The woman bought the material and still saved a large sum of money.

There was a time while living in Chicago that I thought about selling real estate. I was only leaning in that direction because I saw that realtors were making out like bandits. The big deterrent for me was the fact I didn't want to drive people all around town, but more so, I didn't want to spend my nights and weekends working. How ironic, that's exactly what I do today, work endlessly.

With that passing thought, I did have an idea of taking over my father's business and expanding further than he'd ever imagined. Back then, there were benefits to being a woman-owned business or WBE (Women Business Enterprise). This meant that we could acquire government contracts through laws requiring a certain percentage of available work to go directly to women business owners. For years, many companies throughout the nation became 51% owned by women. It was a win-win for many small contracting companies when a woman was seen at the helm.

I was sure I would be taking over the family business. I almost felt as though I had been groomed for it, but then more tragedy was to follow the existing embezzlement. Asbestos Safety was a subsidiary of my father's company. The removal of asbestos was very profitable, but also very costly. We owned a $200K decontamination trailer that companies in this line of work were required to furnish for their employees.

At the end of each work shift an employee would go into the first stall of the enclosed trailer and remove their work clothes. From there they'd step into the second stall to shower, which then led to a third stall to dry off and dress into fresh clothing. It was common practice to leave the decontamination trailer on the job site until the work was completed. Late one night, someone backed a big-rig truck up to the trailer and because the hitch hadn't been locked properly, they were able to drive it off the site. It wasn't insured and was never found. That was just another dagger in an already troubled enterprise.

I mention these different venues of income because I've often heard of entrepreneurs jumping from business to business before ever really giving themselves a chance to be successful at the first. Admittedly, I was this person. Anything I thought I could possibly profit from, I was into it. I must have tried half a dozen multi-level marketing companies before I got a clue that people won't produce if they don't get a check at the end of the week.

When moving to Mission Viejo, California, and after the Costco incident with Donn, I began to seriously consider having my own business. Since previously selling insurance in Chicago, I knew my abilities were strong in this industry and I could achieve great things if left to my own devices.

As a captive agent for Western Southern, I lost every bit of residual income when I'd left the company. That was a big lesson. Everything I'd built went right back to the Divisional Office and the company. This wasn't going to happen to me again. Fool me once, shame on you; fool me twice, shame on me.

Being a captive agent means that everything you do is held captive by the company you work for. If you leave, such as I did, you don't get to take the business with you nor any residual income. It's not that anyone fooled me, but I did learn an extremely valuable lesson. If I'm going to be the little-red-hen and do all the work, my family is going to be the benefactor. I knew that business ownership was in my blood. My father had dropped that information on my siblings and me quite a few times. Now it was time to see what I was made of.

Not everyone is cut-out to lead the way or take the risk of business ownership, but I'd grown up around it and wasn't easily swayed from taking the reigns and galloping toward my goals. The final straw, which wasn't really a bad situation, but more of a reminder, was shortly after working for an insurance agency in California and seeing once again that my commission check didn't represent my hard work. It was time. This was like a spur in my backside and sent me in the final direction. I thoroughly understood that self-employment would be the only road I'd ever walk down again.

I was good at insurance. I wasn't a stranger to picking up the phone and making cold-calls. As a matter of fact, when I first started in the industry with Western Southern, there was no such thing as a paid-for-lead. My first boss set a huge phone book down on my desk and said, "Go for it."

I opened the white pages to the names beginning with A, and one by one, made the calls. At first I was extremely nervous. Though I had a basic script, I wasn't polished enough to sound as though I wasn't reading to the potential client. This was the first road I stumbled across and worked upon improving.

Many people talk themselves out of lucrative careers based solely on the fear of speaking/selling over the phone. I've heard people say things like, "Oh, I could never sell something over the phone," or "Selling is just not in my blood." Then again, "I'd feel like I'm taking someone's money and I'm not comfortable with that."

There are so many excuses people make to avoid being successful in business. Little do most people recognize that they've been selling themselves — practically since birth!

We sell our parents on the fact that we'll be good if they buy us what we want. We sell our friends on the idea that if you do this, then I'll do that. We sell our spouses a bill of goods that we'll be there until death do we part. Okay, some people actually adhere to that, but you get what I'm saying, don't you?

Everything is sold or bought in this world and to tell yourself that you could never do this or that ... well, I hate to say, but I think that's a cop-out.

If you know what your talents are, trust me when I say, the world is waiting for you to expose them. Start out small and don't overwhelm yourself with grandiose expectations. As a matter of fact, those who tackle too much at once, often get so overwhelmed that they end up out of balance and quickly fail. Take the baby steps.

I made the decision to take one step at a time; to learn the process of self-employment. Many people just jump in and go for it, which can also be a good way to start (so you don't talk yourself out of it), though I believe the smarter way is to ease into the first step by actually planning.

There are many books that will help to guide you along the path for success. Many are written by people who have gone before you and want to help others. Though this book is more about inspiring others, there are actual step-by-step guides to assist you. These books offer information such as doing a DBA (Doing Business As), when and how to open a business bank account, advertising, accounting and a complete list of other categorical business terms and procedures. One book that instantly comes to mind are the "how-to" books known as "Idiot's Guide To" … (you pick the subject, they cover it thoroughly).

I wasn't always brave enough to take the steps I needed to grow my business. I worked in my home office for 12 years before really getting the gumption to create a bigger company. Yes, admittedly, the lady you've occasionally seen on TV with the loud lungs was in fear. Now, I channel that fear by creating and accepting challenges that force me to reach new levels.

Sometimes the smallest of creations can help your business the most. While working from my home office, I realized that if I hired someone part-time, to do the paperwork, I could remain on the phone selling.

A really good lesson I learned during the growing years of my business was about micro-managing. It was a hard lesson to bear in the fact that I was too controlling. Yes, I wanted to be in control of my business, but at the same time, if I didn't let go of the reigns little by little, I was sabotaging my own bank account.

If you're in a small office environment, take a peek around the corner of your cubicle; you'll see a place you know most everything about — the business. Also, from this vantage point, if you can visualize well, then for one moment picture yourself as the owner. What if everything you're doing at the office right now was the same thing you would do as a sole proprietor in your own office?

Everyone I know has felt they could do a better job than their boss. Sometimes it's true, but until one gets up and does it, then it's just a dream that lays dormant, unfulfilled.

When I worked for Western Southern and we had the inner-office competitions, though I was often awarded the weekly bonus, there was something more that I wanted. I noticed my boss wasn't truly any better at sales than me, yet his pay was more and the company was taking 50% of my commissions. When I began to scrutinize management and how they handled meetings, business statistics and reports, I knew I could do better, but what I was really doing was putting the wheels in motion for my future.

I asked myself questions like, "Why is my boss still with this company after all these years?" "How long will it take me to be a manager?" "Why would I want to be a manager for someone else's company?" "If I keep doing what I'm doing, will I ever be able to have...?" These thoughts kept swirling in my mind and though I didn't act on them right away, I knew that one day I would.

Finally, I came to the conclusion that managers aren't but a step away from actually being business owners. Sure, they may report to a CEO, but oftentimes they have more insight to the cogs that produce the results — machines, employees, supplies. Granted, the CEO of a company gathers information from each manager or division-head, analyzes it and decides which route to take, but as stated, managers aren't but a step away from doing the same. There's a reason why top managers are often considered first for replacing a retiring CEO ... they've usually proven that they understand the anatomy of the business.

One of the richest men in the world in the early 1900s was Andrew Carnegie. He created a very successful steel mill business, Carnegie Steel Company, through the advice of the managers he hired. He understood that there were men more intelligent than him and had a lot to offer in their respective fields.

Well, this was my thought too. After 12 years in my home office, I began building a business that I could oversee, and guide its direction, while letting others perform in their positions of expertise.

One of the first things I had to learn while working from my home was to keep serious stats (statistics). I learned to keep tabs on the number of calls I made, the types of conversations I was having, re-calling unanswered calls, deals closed, hours of work, leads purchased and an assortment of many other day-to-day business functions. At the end of each week I would have a running tally on my progress. Keeping track of everything is the only way you can tell if you're moving in the right direction.

When we were kids in school we received grades on our work. These grades directed and enabled us to know how we were doing overall. If the grades were low, we knew we had to change our course or direction. Well, it's the same with business ... grade your work!

Keeping statistics can be as simple as taking a piece of graph paper and drawing a line down the left side and a line across the bottom. Where the two points meet at the left is always, in the beginning, zero. If this were a stat on "Cold Calls," you would go from zero upward, counting each line as one. Along the bottom line are your days; starting from the date you begin to the end of the month.

At the end of each day, you record how many calls you made, moving up the chart to perhaps 18. Make a dot on Day One at 18. Come the next day, if you only make 12 calls, then you put a dot on line 12 at Day Two. Then, draw a line from dot 18 down to the dot at 12. You'll see how the direction or flow of calls now stands out clearly.

On another sheet of paper you keep a stat of "Cold Calls Completed," with the same numbering system. A call wouldn't be considered complete if you didn't talk to the potential client.

There are books available about keeping stats on

your business. Some of these books are available in your public library for free. As I said earlier, this book is to inspire and inform you of the possibilities you possess. Keeping stats is so relevant when starting your own company. I would dare to say that those who fail in business didn't keep stats that they could visibly see. If you can't see what each department of your business is doing, how do you know if they're being successful?

Stats should be kept on every measurable part of a business and is more important to your success than anything I can recommend. If you have employees, they need to keep stats on their progress and turn them in weekly.

How many networking functions did you go to? How many times this week did you start a conversation with someone about your particular business? How much reading did you do to increase your knowledge concerning your business? How many seminars did you go to this month/year? How many weeks in a row did you have stats that were spiraling down? How many weeks were your stats going upward?

Even though I worked alone while at home, I knew where my metaphorical ship was heading. Can you imagine if you were an admiral of a huge Navy destroyer with a good size crew and you wanted to go from Port A to Port B, but you didn't know how much fuel your ship used per hour or day? Information needs to be collected and analyzed if one expects a successful journey.

Knowing how to keep statistics is all fine and dandy, but those stat sheets will do absolutely no good without a well designed plan for your business. My plan to own an insurance agency included that I was to be a sole proprietor (sole owner of the business). It was a definitive decision that there were to be no options for partnerships. I didn't want someone that could take 50% of the profit for doing less than that amount of the work.

Well-laid plans offer you the knowledge of what needs to be done before you spend one cent. If money for funding is a problem, then there are options of having silent partners. This is usually a person that will loan you money for a declared period of time with an attached percentage added to the return. They may also want a share of your profits. It all depends on the deal you make — never give away the farm. Haggle until you're out of breath.

Silent partners should never have a say regarding how you run your business, hence the name, Silent Partner. They will expect a good return for taking a risk on you. In my opinion, this is the only type of partner to have when it comes to business.

If one does opt for a partner, there really needs to be a lot of groundwork done beforehand. You should have an attorney draw up the contract between your partner/s and you and stipulate exactly what is expected from each partner/s, no exceptions. There have been many successful businesses with two or more partners, but these were people that could put their egos aside and do what was really right for the company and its employees.

If you're like me, and feel that others will work to take advantage of you, then going solo is highly recommended … follow your true self, follow your gut.

When finding a business loan, I suggest going to a bank. Depending on your credit, they'll work with you and help to make your dreams a reality. I suggest small business loans from banks rather than family members. This way, if you fail and can't pay back the bank, family functions will still be bearable. There is a reason people say, "Never loan money to family members or friends."

If you don't heed the advice and you still borrow money from a family member, then make sure you do every single thing in your power to pay them back if your business folds.

I have respect for my employees and I'd hate to lose them to another company or become a competitor to me, but I'd completely back them in their decision to try. There will always be more than enough work in the insurance industry. How could anyone hold another back from wanting to better their life? Another big lesson I learned and truly had to take to heart — sometimes I get the client and sometimes I don't — that's business.

Employees that step away from any company shouldn't be feared as competition, but as respectable persons making their way in society. I never want to stop someone's drive.

Through personal experience of playing both sides of the fence, employee and business owner, when it comes to being self-employed there are a couple of things I'd suggest. Regardless of the field you're in, if you want to be self-employed, then start taking notes and deciphering how the company you work for operates. If you don't have experience in your field of choice, then try obtaining a position in a company where you can learn or perfect your talents. Don't re-invent the wheel. Get the experience firsthand.

There's always going to be a learning curve when in business for yourself. I've had clients that lead me down one path regarding an insurance policy and just before signing on the line, they insure with another agent elsewhere. It can make being in business frustrating and the most you can do in this type of situation is to bite your lip and move on. Chalk it up as experience.

I once gave a lead to a fellow agent while at Western Southern Insurance with the understanding that we would split the commission. When it came time for the guy to pay out my share, he refused and said he needed the money. I went to my boss who refused to get involved. Hello, lip — prepare yourself. Not everyone you deal with will have the same ethics as you. The sooner you realize this, the easier life will be.

Now you know why I suggest going solo in business. It's a difficult road to hoe when one puts out more than others and it's a metaphorical garden that will never bloom beautifully if everyone involved is not tending the soil properly.

Though I tend to believe that insurance is one of the greatest industries to be involved in, having suggested it to many people, I understand that not everyone can jump instantly into being self-employed.

I don't suggest people dabble when it comes to a career. If you happen to work a day job and want to do something in the evening, be professional about it. To me, this means that within two hours of completing one job, I'm starting a serious drive with my second — which would be my own business, if possible.

If you carefully strategize and create a professional standard for yourself by keeping proper statistics, there will come a time when you can look at your stats and project a pattern, cycle or flow. This will enable you to make decisions regarding a future of full-time self-employment, or during a lull, to take a break and visit with family and friends.

Dabbling, in my mind, is a sign that one is not sure what they want to do. If you work in an office during the day, but sew clothing on the side for a few extra bucks – you're dabbling. Perhaps you don't believe that your sewing business could make you enough money to replace the day job. The questions I have: are you keeping stats on your sewing? Are you promoting your sewing? If not, then you're dabbling.

It's the same with other businesses. If you're working from home and not seriously shut off from the TV, the kids and a blanket of intrusions that keep you from racking up serious statistics each week, you're dabbling. I too, had to understand this and when I decided to be completely professional, my business stats took off like a rocket ship heading to Mars.

There are many things I learned along the way while increasing my business that I'd like to share. Even though we may be in totally different fields, it doesn't mean these ideas can't be applied to your occupation.

Chaos will inevitably show up in some fashion in

your life or business. In the next chapter, "Breaking Out of the Pack," I explain how I dealt with Chaos through Control. It's always easy to recognize, and rarely, if ever, willingly controlled.

Chapter Six

Breaking out of the Pack

Chaos and Control

Breaking out of the pack is what one does when they can no longer sit idly by and watch the world get the better of them. For 12 long years I worked from my home office, and though I did well by keeping my overhead really low, I was limiting myself and my income.

I had to make surefire plans to break from the pack. It's not that I was working with any particular group of insurance agents that I needed to break away from, but more so, I had to break out of the comfort zone I'd let myself seep in to.

At the time, I'd grown my business to the extent that it could go. If I wanted more, I knew I had to move the business out of the home and into an office building.

I'd like to recall the idea that I was cool and calm about moving to an office space, a place where I'd be spending money on overhead that wasn't creating equity, such as my home. I was anything but cool or calm. I was in great fear and really didn't want the added expense.

I searched quite a bit before shelling out $1200 for two sublet offices in an Executive Realty Building. I pondered, lost sleep, walked and talked to myself while trying to figure out how I would pay for this added expense. Finally, I figured out that I would have to make a few more sales per month to cover the cost, so I decided to take the personal challenge and set forth to work away from my house.

Once I was in the new space, I quickly learned some very valuable lessons. Yes, it was nice to have an available conference room where I could meet with my clients, but sharing the place with a bunch of realtors had its downside. Some clients became confused and would ask if I was a realtor or an insurance agent. There was also a lot of chit-chatting amongst the realtors throughout the whole office floor, it sounded like a hen-house and was a major distraction. It was then that I began to recognize and understand chaos and also learned that I could have control.

The impetus to move to a new location was when one client too many asked the realtor vs. insurance question. I couldn't have that. I didn't feeling like I could get the privacy needed to conduct business in a professional manner. There was a newly-built office building not far from my home where I established my business and began to build my brand.

Just when you think you've controlled chaos, trust me when I say, it will always find a way to present itself in other forms or venues. If I were to offer advice to anyone regarding chaos and control, I'd tell them — just expect it. Think back throughout your life and how many times you've experienced some form of chaos.

As you may recall from an earlier chapter regarding my marriage, I had too much chaos. In my divorce, I was awarded a portion of Mike's salary as support for the kids, but not long after the court's decision and Mike leaving my father's company, the support stopped. I could have taken Mike back to court and fought until I was blue in the face, all the while creating more chaos, wasting money and time.

As stated, chaos comes in many forms. I just choose to recognize when it's happening and more often than not, I make the decision to step aside. In this respect, I'm in control.

Chaos can sometimes be a juggling act and be seen in

the form of one's work, kids, school schedules, mortgage, car payment, credit cards and more. People have the choice to willingly throw their hands up in angst, or they could plan and diligently get down to brass tacks, making things work in their favor. The ball/control is always in your court.

At times, I understand chaos to be my friend. I get to learn things quite quickly. I'm not always happy at the given moment, but when the dust settles I've dealt with reality and regained control.

Perhaps, breaking away from the pack should be rewritten into breaking away with the stats. In reality, there isn't much else that matters when it comes to knowing where your business has been or where it's heading. Chaotic stats define an absence in communication.

I explained how I found my purpose, direction and then created drive. Well, when you're trying to increase your business even further, it's time to look and revise what your employees are doing.

I constantly remind my employees that I treat them fairly and expect the same in return. If I leave the office for a week, I need to know that people are doing what's expected of them, if not more. Sure, I have an office manager that I thoroughly trust, but if I'm out of town and I happen to call the office, I never want to hear a phone that keeps ringing.

What I'm leading to is this, when you're an established business and you've decided to take the next step toward growth of your company, then the most important ingredients you'll add are the people you hire. Having more employees can lead to having more chaos, but this too, can be controlled.

Working for a company long ago, I was lucky to observe two employees basically doing the same job. One employee would go to the boss with information that had been requested. The second employee went to the same boss with requested information, but brought the boss more information that was pertinent to a well informed and complete decision.

Obviously, the employee covering all the bases raised the bar in professionalism, but more importantly, cut costs through time saved.

When you find an employee that brings not just the bread, but the butter too, and then before you can ask, they hand you a knife for the spread — hold on to them. They're worth their weight in gold.

If your business isn't to the level that you can afford to hire personnel full time, then you can always look for independent outside sources. I've always made sure that the professionals I'm opening my business to have a business license, and are insured or bonded. Even when they've come recommended by a mutual friend, if I don't know them personally, I still have them checked out.

I always adhere to finding the right people for the right job. I follow my gut feeling, but at the same time, I do a background check on each prospective employee or outside source. I can't emphasize this enough. If someone is going to have access to my books, account numbers and vital information, it's imperative that I know everything possible about them. Never skimp on the cost of knowing who you're hiring, because it could cost you ten times or more than what you would have spent. Case in point, my father thought he knew the secretary that robbed him blind.

Of course, there are no fail-safes. People can be honest one minute and corrupt the next. It's up to you to pay attention to what is happening in your business, even if you've hired someone to watch everything for you. Who's watching the watcher?

With all the positions to be covered in my business, hiring a good Controller was one of the best investments I've made. A good Controller is there to help keep chaos at bay when it comes to your finances — payroll, taxes, banking and an array of other monetary needs. If you're doing these jobs to save a few bucks, believe it or not, you're possibly costing yourself thousands of dollars more than necessary.

You may pay a few more dollars for self-employed professionals, but by the same token, you're not covering their employee taxes, health benefits or any other dollar absorbed through the overhead costs of being in business.

Let's talk about Controllers for a moment. Other than your office manager, I'm not sure who would be more important to a small or medium size business. They're not just there to oversee the books, but they also help to look into the future. I don't know how many times I've come up with a plan and my Controller looked at me in silence. I could instantly see her eyes calculating where the decimal point belonged and when she sums everything up — Whamo! She hits me with the figures I'll need to pull off the next venture.

With my Controller and my stats, we're able to see cycles or divisions in the business that may be lacking. By the end of a Monday morning staff meeting, everyone knows the objectives and how to handle any slack toward the company goals.

Through diligence, I keep business costs at a minimum, but there is no way around certain expenses. You can negotiate a good price on advertising or accounting, but my industry doesn't allow for bartering.

When I settle on a goal I want to achieve in the next few months, I get together with my Controller and we decide the actions necessary to bring up the amount of revenue. Usually it's just a matter of motivating the sales reps to put more umph in their drive, but just the same, I also work to increase my output.

Speaking of output, I heard this line, "Outflow equals inflow." Visiting the Chamber of Commerce meetings, sending out direct mailers, joining networking groups, making phone calls and countless other avenues of getting information into the hands of your prospects is the outflow. The more you continuously outflow, eventually the inflow will happen. Just a reminder, there should be a stat sheet set up for each and every type of outflow/inflow thing you do.

(I'm not the most successful businesswoman in the world when it comes to being rated by Forbes, but I have reached a very good level thus far. Many who read this material may already know some of the things I'm speaking of, but just the same, there are many that don't. There are things I will say that some may have learned long ago, and they may never have decided to put into practice until now. My goal here is to inspire others to consider the possibilities of having their own business, increasing their business or fine tuning what they have already.)

Another great way to break away from the pack is to go back and look at your original business plans. Occasionally they offer bits of information you may or may not have used, but are applicable to a present situation. Hopefully, you had plans and weren't just shooting from the hip.

If you've stored your plans and past stats, you'll find there's nothing better than to see records of you making $50K in your first year, then by year three or four, the same stat shows $150K. Seeing this type of information is very stimulating and can help create the necessary emotions to shift into overdrive.

At the start of your business venture you may not have thought about becoming a brand, a household name. Just for the sake of knowledge, some people confuse a brand with a logo. Yes, logos can help establish a brand by public recognition, but a brand is really what a company states they are committed to or hold to be sacred within.

A company that takes complete responsibility for its product and makes sure the customer is always number one builds a strong, dependable and sought-after brand.

In the old days, branding was used to recognize ownership of property such as cattle. Now a brand is often recognized by an insignia or logo, which, in turn, offers instant recognition by a consumer. Through an easily identified logo, corporations made the declaration that they were offering the absolute best in products or services. This increased their share of the market if consumers were happy with their purchase. Recommendations through word-of-mouth will always be a company's best advertisement.

When starting Coto Insurance, my main objective was to make sure that people were covered in case of death, illness or unforeseen catastrophe. Though I make a good living in the insurance business, I could truly care less about the money over someone's health or life.

I've delivered too many death benefit checks and have taken many deep breaths knowing how blessed I am to not have experienced extreme tragedy. When I hug a woman in bereavement and know that she and her kids are financially taken care of, it calms my own heart to know I helped, even if I feel in a small way.

I have a slogan I use, "Where clients are family," and it correlates with my brand — it's about being there for people. I've been recognized and appreciated for my actions. Making someone understand why they need life insurance is not the easiest thing to do.

Many people just see themselves with less money each month. Insuring young adults is especially difficult because they have a concept of invincibility. Until people stop to think about it, they don't realize that there is a 100% chance they will die, we just don't know when. How will your death and loss of income as the breadwinner affect your family?
When tragedy does occurs, it's then that the client understands my purpose, drive and concern — my brand.

What is your brand? Is it in alignment with your purpose? One of the biggest realizations I've had regarding a brand is that it's absolutely never about the bottom dollar. It is always about servicing and making sure others are taken care of in a very respectful manner.

Of the many aspects involved in breaking away, I want to continue by informing the new entrepreneurs, but also the established sole proprietors, how important it is that they make sure to separate their business revenue from their personal account.

The reason I bring this up now is because while breaking away in business you will need to really have a grip on your finances. I've met many self-employed people that haven't separated business dollars from personal dollars. Nothing will end your lifestyle quicker than poor financing.

We've all heard about people who completely funded their business through the use of credit cards. To me, this is a crazy thing to do. Though some have been successful, most have not, and of those, they're left with maxed out credit cards and major financial problems.

I'd suggest that if you're serious about business, then you will have a well written out list of your personal bills and another list for your business costs, your overhead. Any knowledge short of full disclosure will catch up with you at some point.

Banking will be a major player in your business and establishing a line-of-credit, whether you need it right now or not, it's very important. A good line of credit allows you to expand staff, produce more products or cover anything unaccounted for when times are tough. If you didn't get the memo in the beginning of the book about my father, never put your home up for collateral.

If you've kept good records, then the bank isn't necessarily doing business with you, so much as, it's doing business with your Company XYZ. If you're incorporated, then the bank will go after the business in the case of default. This is one reason why you always separate your personal finances from your business.

I used a part of my line-of-credit to design and move into an office that clients or employees could feel comfortable in. The atmosphere is sort of a home away from home. It's so comfortable that my employees are okay with working into the late hours, sometimes forgetting that it's an actual office.

Though I used a portion of my credit line to build a comfortable office, I also used it to boost my business — Internet services, obtain new sales reps, purchase more leads.

It's nice to be able to create a peaceful image, but if I hadn't used an equal portion of the money to create more business than image, well, things would get out of balance, and we all know what happens when the teeter won't totter.

Having a line-of-credit during an economic downturn, such as the country has been experiencing, enabled me to increase my business while others are shaking their heads and wondering how to stay afloat. The businesses that succeed during hard times are those that have back-up plans and are prepared to market themselves extensively.

If your business has had problems, I hope it wasn't due to cutting off the flow of information through direct communication via the telephone, emails or any type of advertising. Remember, outflow equal inflow.

Yes, times do get hard and the bigger you are in business the harder it is to stay afloat, unless you're prepared. My staff and I couldn't be happier if our competition closes their doors at sunset. Because we're willing to stick it out and put in the added hours, we fill the void. I want to be creating when others are quitting. That's drive!

You should know, based on your stats and production, what you can do now and also what's possible in the next three months. At this level of breaking away you'll need to put more pressure on your employees to produce. I know this sounds kind of bad, but in a moment you'll understand why it's not.

There is an 80/20 rule in the business world that states 20% of the people are doing the work or producing the end results. In my industry there is a 90/10 rule. This means 10% of the people are producing the end results and the rest are barely contributing. By keeping stats on each individual in your company, you will always know what percentage the employee falls under, and you will know who you should put the pressure on to produce.

Once a sales rep starts to see their commissions increase, it becomes incredibly motivating. Money does have a way of making people reach for more. Well, if you're a leader in your company, it's not out of line for you to expect results from the other 90%.

Can this 90/10 rule be considered a stat of chaos? Can it be controlled? Could you imagine where your company would break away to, if the stat said 60 out of 100 people were producing incredible results? What if you created a stat on the amount of people you had in sales producing positions, and then worked on bringing each individual's stat considerably higher? Think of the possibilities of what the combination of stats and pressure can do for one's lifestyle.

Create competition within your firm — bonuses, vacations for two, sporting events, sending an employee's kids on an incredible adventure. There are many ways to motivate people without their knowledge that you want more for them. As a boss, always take a personal interest in creating more for your employees. If they just can't rise to the level needed, it's unfortunate, but you have to weigh their value to the company.

A very successful friend said to me recently, "You don't know what success looks like until you have it — lack of sleep, lack of family time, lack of exercise." I have each of these and I have lost a few friends along the way. I came to a point in my life that even though I enjoy friendships, I'm having an incredible affair with my business, and like an artist lost in a slab of clay or a beautiful mosaic, I'm on purpose and creating life-sustaining results, not only for me, but for hundreds of others.

Everything you did when you started your business must be amped up considerably when in the breaking away mode. Your emergency slush fund needs to be bigger, your advertising dollars need to go further and your social skills need to be spot-on. With each of these items, you also need to know what they really entail. When I say that your advertising dollar needs to go further, I'm saying you need to haggle over price more than you've done in the past. You have to know exactly where you're really getting the biggest bang for the buck. Is it in direct mailers, buying more leads, social networking in the Chamber of Commerce?

If you've spent your share of advertising dollars with one agency, and if they haven't already offered a discount for customer loyalty, it's not all that uncommon to let them know how you feel. They realize that there are companies that put out quality work for less. It sounds very cut-throat, but just the same, this is business and you're trying to break away. Every single dollar you can save in one arena can be worth much more in the coffers/slush fund for future growth.

Breaking away doesn't mean you become ruthless, but it does mean that you'll be growing a new skin. It's a bit thicker, and interestingly enough, sends a direct message of strength to those who will now understand that it's not "business as usual."

"Doing the same thing will produce the same results." This statement is posted in my office as a constant reminder that I must change as the need arises. You may recognize a statement close to it, "Insanity is doing something the same way, over and over, and expecting a different result."

As you grow and break your own stat records you will have to change; it's inevitable. Believe it or not, you get to decide which changes you'll make when it comes to your personal or business life. It's not always easy to separate the two, and occasionally your business will follow you home and try to ransack the place. When this happens, you'll know the teeter has tottered. You'll need to back up and take a long, hard look in the mirror. In Section Three, "Celebrity," I share a personal experience that made me a bit sick. It was only then that I realized I had to change the skin I was covered with.

I've spoken a lot about chaos and controlling your business. What I haven't dealt with is what happens when emotions get involved during chaotic moments. When things are unbalanced, it's not always easy to understand exactly what's happening. You may sense things are out of place or not going right, but the chaos may be low level, flying slightly under the radar. Oftentimes, it's not until the dam breaks that you can find the source to your problems.

Having weekly meetings may help to keep chaos at bay, but those meetings can also fuel the chaos to become a full-blown fire.

Either way, it's okay. Full-blown fires in a meeting room means there has been chaos sauntering around, and now that it's ignited it must be dealt with.

There have been many times that I let my emotions get involved. I've been seen ranting and raving about some things that weren't going smoothly. I've learned that when I'm in a slight rage about something, it's because I've been triggered.

As an example, during one of the shows a limousine company sent a small mini-van to take my family and our luggage to the airport. I had a complete communication with the company the day before. I was very specific that my family and I were going to Europe and I wanted a 12-passenger limo-bus stocked with mimosas, croissants, fresh bagels and cheese. I told them that it should be capable of storing a lot of luggage that we were taking with us to the airport.

Unannounced, chaos was slowly creeping into the scene. When the mini-van showed up and not the limo-bus, I instantly thought I was somehow being punked by the show's producers and that the limo was just around the corner. When I learned that it wasn't coming, after having confirmed exactly what I wanted only 24 hours earlier, chaos was ready to step into the open.

I thought of how unprofessional this transportation

company had been and my emotions were triggered. Chaos was completely revealed and I let my emotions get too involved. I went from being a busy woman trying to get everything organized to a raging, angry woman in a matter of seconds.

As simple as it is, the emotion had been triggered by a similar incident long ago, a communication that had gone bad, but was handled the same way as this incident, with anger. The part not so simple is to know when you're about to be triggered.

It's when we've been triggered, through boardroom meetings or in our daily lives, that we can piece our past together and solve some of life's mysteries. When we allow ourselves to express an emotion of anger, it's then we can look to find similar incidences that make up this emotion. It's a chance to not go down the same road time after time, or to be insane. Once I break this bond with that certain past incident and recognize it and where it started, chaos goes away.

If you're asking what emotions have to do with breaking away? Let me ask you this: are people always rational when they get angry about something? No, most people are not. Keeping a clear and unemotional mind is a big key to breaking away.

Yelling at an employee that may have done something wrong is never the answer to solving a problem. Yelling only comes when the emotion has been triggered. Being in charge of your emotions is critical to making correct decisions when trying to break away.

No, I'm not a psychologist or any other form of doctor, but I have learned some things that I wish to express and share with others, so they too, may contemplate their life and possibly come to some conclusions that ease their conscience and enable them to move forward.

Have you ever metaphorically been carrying a hundred pounds of luggage on your back and then when you were enlightened by someone's words, that bag was gone and life got noticeably easier? Well, once again, that's my purpose in life. I want to share the things I'm learning so that others can be happier and safe.

To sum up chaos and control, I would like you, the reader, to know that I have never felt as though I am perfect. I don't believe chaos and control are bad in any way, but allow us insight into our ability to cope in this life. They really are just two significant parts of life that enable us to keep the teeter tottering.

Reach out and create a stat sheet for your life. You'll be amazed at your accomplishments when you can visually see the records of your progress.

In the next chapter, "Breaking Through, Creating Affluence," I share some of the things I did while breaking away, that also led to me creating a bigger and better lifestyle for myself and those around me. Join me — it's just a page away.

Chapter Seven

Pushing Through

Creating Affluence

When you reach the milestone that marks your hard-won affluence, buy yourself something amazing. It should reek of wealth. I boasted quite a bit about a Rolex I had recently purchased. I've bought my share of Jimmy Choo shoes and Armani business suits, but these are things I believe every businesswoman should own. On the other hand (no pun intended), a Rolex? Buying this watch is not in everyone's taste or budget, but I knew it made a statement — it's a quick dissertation on the word "accomplishment"!

I live in a beautiful home on two acres in an expensive private community, I drive an elegant Mercedes Benz, I'm escorted to special events via limousine services and I love every minute of it. This is not to brag, but to express that the work I do, the long hours I've committed and the drive to make it happen, is all anyone really needs to create a life of affluence.

Working smart instead of hard wasn't always in my vocabulary. Admittedly, I can be a stubborn woman. I have learned many of my lessons the hard way – try, try, try, and fail, fail, fail … but, get up, revise and do it again.

I never could have reached the level I have without the hundreds of people beside me - sales reps, mentors, clients, friends, my husband and kids, and even the chaotic times. These are the real reasons I'm considered successful.

Every bit of my life has come to fruition because of my choices and how I handled any given situation. I'm sure the same goes for your life as well.

How you handle any given situation is imperative to creating affluence. Have you ever dodged a bill collector? If so, you need to recognize it as a red flag; you're not on top of your financial game. I was taught to be responsible for my bills first. You may have heard that you should always pay yourself and then take care of what's due. Well, to be frank, you already paid yourself first when you agreed to use a service such as a credit card.

Don't get me wrong. If you work for yourself or a company and you can put money into a 401k or other investment tool first, go for it! Just be sure that you have enough left in your check to pay the bills. It will never make sense to save money at an 8% interest rate when a credit card is costing you 19% or more.

So, am I talking about creating affluence or obtaining wealth? Actually, both! If done correctly, one does beget the other.

I didn't do anything unusual to become affluent. Millions of people around the world are doing the same thing I am - taking one step at a time while understanding the ramifications if we neglect the steps in any way. An example would be: I worked in my home office for 12 years and was in fear about growing bigger in business. The costs I'd incur by having an office-space were frightening. While I may have saved on overhead and invested that money into my portfolio, I was also not taking the proper steps to succeed on a larger scale.

Success is sometimes as scary as failure and both seem to loom on the horizon. I watched my dad's business take a major blow through betrayal, by not being more watchful. I saw my marriage fail because I didn't partner with some-one that wanted the same future as me.

I was lucky to have remarried someone with the same values, but quickly realized I had to continue to take charge of my life.

Even as I enjoy my success, I'm determined to maintain and enhance my lifestyle.

While banks are failing and other insurance agencies are trying desperately to stay afloat, I've increased my business by over 70% in the past three years.

I keep my focus on my purpose and continue to drive myself. I intend to exceed my wildest expectations. I truly am hooked on beating my personal best and my next quarter projections. I keep an eye on the statistics and will know during any given day, week, month or year, if I'm on course.

The way I start my day is essential to how it will flow. I don't usually want to leave my cozy bed. I lie still for a moment and visualize what I want to have happen. Then, at some point, I kick into gear and I'm out of bed ready to attack a bootcamp class or the day's oncoming schedule.

How does this create affluence? Well, when I'm in the gym or outside at the bootcamp class, I get to relieve myself of the stress that does build up. Working out early in the morning allows me to face the day with exuberance and confidence. I feel alive. There's a bounce in my step. I make better, more positive choices. I tackle everything with discipline, enthusiasm and lots of energy. This mindset allows me to reach for things that others may not.

There are mornings when I can't get to the gym and I must deal with priorities. I'm okay with this. I know I'll be back at it soon and I'm not avoiding it, I'm just temporarily preoccupied with more important things.

You might be thinking that there are many affluent businessmen and women that have never stepped foot in a gym, and that the gym has nothing to do with affluence. True, to a degree. I can guarantee that those people that are experiencing affluence in their business have their own secrets to staying motivated and relieving stress.

It may not be the gym, but they have a time, place and pursuit that sustains them. Perhaps they read, walk, swim or even just sit in their favorite chair while sipping a cup of hot tea. They create a time and place to let their mind solve problems, to sooth anxiety. I've often lost myself while on the treadmill! My mind wanders while my heart rate accelerates. Step by step, I leave stress behind. While walking in place, I've moved on to the next challenge.

What is affluence? How does one know when they're in it? Well, to me, it's when my numbers are off the charts, when my reps exceed their quotas, when I have to set new challenges for everyone to beat their personal best.

What I do next is more important than anything else. I observe what the action was that created affluence and then reinforce those actions. Do them again!

Affluence is often thought of as a word describing wealth or riches, but it is also defined as an abundant supply. When I started Coto Insurance, I had only one sales rep and that was me. After I had two and then three reps, a little light went off and I realized that if I could do this good with just a few reps, then why couldn't I duplicate what I'm doing with 10, 20, 30, 300, 700 or 1000s .... Do you see where I'm going with this?

Today, Coto Insurance has approximately 700 agents across the country. A little over 300 of them are active on a daily basis (remember the 90/10 rule). Acquiring this many agents didn't happen overnight, but it seems like it did.

Only five years ago I was working from my home office with one part-time assistant. I didn't have an official, website, agent certification school or the reps and staff that I have today. I didn't even have a business degree, but I did have the drive. I went out and did what had to be done. I took my solid business plan and ventured forth into the world. I remembered a quote: "If you can believe it, you can achieve it." It's true! I'm living proof!

Your business plan doesn't have to be elaborate; it just has to be realistic, meaning that you've thought through your goals, your strategy and tactics, that you understand how much money, time and effort it will take to get your business launched. Then, you should probably double all of your estimates. Be frugal, be visionary, be determined, be relentless - that's how you become affluent.

Eventually, everything plateaus. Affluence wanes and you must find opportunities to create another burst of business through additional products or services, the purchase of other businesses or expanding on your target market. You must always do more to attain higher levels, not to mention keep what you've already built.

I'm now working to reach a wider audience through radio. Through my ads and personal appearances, I've secured new leads. Currently, I'm providing information to help people build or retain their wealth, keeping them financially secure. My brand is now becoming naturally known and I'm seen as an expert in my field.

I am always on the lookout for the next business opportunity. Even though I'm affluent, I have to keep my business growing, my staff employed and my drive nurtured.

There isn't one day of traveling that I'm not on the phone to the office. While on a plane to my next destination, I'm busy working on my laptop. I can't count the number of times over the past few years that fans or flight attendants who know of me, have politely tried to tell me, "take a break." They don't understand the pressure I'm under to make sure I hit my deadline for radio shows, or to be prepared for a speaking engagement. I'm relied on to be sharp - day in and day out. As Charles Barkley once said, "I'll take a break when I'm dead."

At this level of business, there's always so much more to do. I'm hiring more office personnel, adding more agents, buying more leads and reinvesting money back into the business. When I'm in a state of affluence I'm paying off debt and upgrading technological tools that empower employees to reach more people.

Not only do we have inner-office competitions, but occasionally, I choose a place to bring agents for a two-day bootcamp training session, enabling them to be more productive, to get that little something extra missing in their game. At the end of the second day, I charter a bus, hire a band and invite everyone to my home for a Mexican fiesta. Can you say woo-hoo? I can and I do!

I love my staff and I truly feel honored that many sales reps have come from other insurance agencies to work with me at Coto Insurance. From what I've learned, some of these reps weren't being serviced or treated fairly by their previous employer. I always take care of my reps. I refer leads to them and give them the training and incentive to do well for themselves and the company. That's how the level of affluence is attained.

If you find that you're having a hard time getting to the next big level of business growth, I suggest you talk to your colleagues, mentors, confidants. Speak with anyone who has some insight into your type of business, your stage of growth or perhaps has experienced a similar roadblock at some point.

Just talking about your concerns is illuminating. You'll see alternatives, options, new approaches that'll help you see beyond the obstacles.

In a recent conversation with a businessman, I helped him realize that a 4% yearly increase in business wasn't nearly enough to ensure his company's survival. He needed to take drastic actions toward reaching a wider customer base to increase his percentages. I'm pretty certain he hadn't been keeping or relying on stats - big mistake!

When you're in business, a 4% yearly increase is like barely keeping your head above water level. If you want to enjoy affluence, anything less than an 8-10% yearly increase will threaten your company's solvency.

If you keep good records about what works and what doesn't work, what generates income and lowers costs, you'll be able to pinpoint exactly what needs to be done in the years to come.

If you hired three star sales reps last year and got a 10% profit with this move, then do it again this year. Again, correct actions will always stand out if you've kept good records of your past actions.

Staying at a level of affluence means that one must track everything. Track your in-house sales reps and everything they do: number of calls, closed deals, productive hours worked. Anyone that works for you can have a stat sheet applied to them. Know your business and who is being productive.

Tracking your costs is important. Every dollar spent on some outside source is a dollar missing from your profit margin. Add those dollars up over a 12-month period and decide just how much you like that product or service. Fresh flowers delivered weekly to your office may be nice, but what could you do with the $1500 saved annually? This money, along with other savings, invested wisely over a 20-year period can make a huge difference in one's retirement plan.

Re-explore your company notes. What was happening in the years of solid growth that you no longer do? Did you have special or exceptional employees? Were your overhead costs lower? Do your notes reveal why your company may have declined? Did you hire people that didn't last? Did you keep people that weren't productive? There is always an answer to every question. To create affluence, one must be honest and do their research through notes.

Keeping good records is an important part of communication which is essential to obtaining success. Every employee must have input and buy-off on corporate goals, best practices and productivity expectations. Stats are the way much of our progress is measured. The numbers don't lie; they present a graphic depiction of sales and costs in an easy-to-understand manner. You can quickly compare the numbers year to year and the rep's output at every turn.

Mistakes are a great way to understand when communication has gone awry. A recognized mistake means something was lost in translation. Never assume. Always clarify, reiterate and recheck.

Regardless of whether it's business or on a personal level, every problem that exists is from a communication. When a child brings home a D on their paper, it's a communication problem. When a sales rep can't close a deal, it's a communication problem. When a business is in decline, again, it's about communication.

Let me be clear here, pushing through is not the same as breaking away. When you reach a certain level of affluence you are up against a much greater wall, that at times, seems impenetrable. This is where the real fine-tuning must be done. No bulldozers, no explosives, but precise evaluations. Is your website working efficiently? Are your employees properly trained to do their best? Is every dollar working to make you more? Do you have people in the field collecting future leads or creating more buzz about your company? Do you know exactly how much money came in and how much went out? Are there any expenses you can cut to increase the bottom line? Only you can ask the right questions for your business.

I try to attend an industry convention at least once a month. My business can't thrive in a vacuum. When I get home, I study my notes and see what new ideas may help my business. I must stay up to date. I can't lag behind the competition.

Is your financial planner going to industry conventions? Are they up to date on the latest information and changes to money management or insurance issues? You should be knowledgeable about anything concerning your business and finances, especially when they're in the hands of another.

I work the conventions, introducing myself to speakers or trend influencers, recognized achievers. I soak up every bit of new information. I initiate follow-up meetings and I build business and personal friendships. I get the opportunity to see what other business owners are doing to succeed. I also get to look at my business from the outside and gain a new perspective. There is always a road we haven't explored, but should be moving toward.

Sharing information with your business peers is a vital part of growth for any industry. Cutting off that flow is detrimental to your own bottom line. Just because you make the information available doesn't mean everyone will utilize it. More power to them if they do.

When I get a call from someone who wants to pick my brain, I try to find the time to meet. I've had mentors along the way and I believe I have a responsibility to pass on my good fortune. What if one act of kindness could send a person on a journey that meant a better life for his or her family? I like keeping the flow of success going, sharing what I've learned with others. It's part of my purpose.

You may feel that you don't owe anyone anything. It's always a personal choice. I don't praise those who help nor do I condemn those who don't.

I would say that one major reason I've made it to my level of affluence is because I've never expected anyone to give me anything. I have an understanding that there is more than a 50% chance of incurring divorce and there's a 100% chance that either my spouse or I are going to die, one before the other. If I put all my eggs in their basket, what will I have if they decide to leave or worse yet, tragically die? I have to rely on myself, not a husband, not anyone.

Through the years, I've known people who planned for emergencies and those who didn't. It's taught me an incredible lesson about being self-sufficient. I love my kids and my spouse, but they will never have to care for me if something happens, making me unable to function on my own.

Perhaps my fear of becoming dependent on someone else is why I'm driven to protect the financial security of others. I will maintain my affluence and retain my independence.

I have many goals I've yet to accomplish. If I keep the drive I have now at least another 10 years, I will reach the level of affluence that I admire in some of the world's wealthiest. My personality won't allow me to dabble in business, I'm all in. I believe you too can find your talents and your purpose, kick in your drive and be successful. Start today!

Remember, I was once afraid of working away from my home office. I took a deep breath, exhaled and moved into an office building. Just keep breathing. Keep achieving. I constantly remind myself, "I think I can do this. I can be good at this." Sure enough, I am good at what I do.

"Every successful person was once a beginner."
Author Unknown

Chapter Eight

Pinnacles

Manifestations of Thought
Measures of Success

Pinnacles are the manifestations of thoughts in direct alignment with desires.

When we're successful at something, rarely do we take the time to realize it all started with a simple thought.

There have been many pinnacles in my life. I'm sure you have also experienced many in yours. As the statement starting this chapter declared, it's when we're in alignment with our desires that we manifest our thoughts into reality. In the last chapter I mentioned that I couldn't help but to be successful at what I was doing. I took each step necessary to reach my pinnacles.

We know some pinnacles will come automatically, like raising children, it's common knowledge that they will one day be grown and have moved out of the house (if you taught them well).

In business, pinnacles come sparingly. They do eventually happen if you keep reaching for your desires and work to follow well laid-out plans.

As you recall, I used to work alone from my home. I wasn't sure how I was going to expand and make more money. The only thing I had going for me was my mind and the thought that I could eventually do whatever I truly wanted.

There was a point when I was looking at my personal stats and I said something to the effect of, "Is there a way to make more money in this business?" That's basically it. I wanted to make more money. The second question I asked was, "How can I make more money?" Then the last, "What should I do?"

I put the questions in the back of my mind and went back to work. I figured the answers would come to me later. Then, little by little, information was delivered through unexpected sources. Things began to make sense. I observed how quickly my mind came up with pictures of past experiences in this industry. Each of the offices where I'd previously worked had a considerable number of employees.

In my mind, I saw an office of people and then I saw myself. The visualizations didn't guide me to any certain figure representing a boss or manager. If anyone else had seen the picture in my brain, as though it were a scene on TV, they never could have known whose office it was. My imagination made this my office.

I began to visualize myself being in control of my own firm. At that very moment, thought was beginning to manifest in the real world. You could actually liken it to having a baby. You're with your spouse and you make the decision to have children (the manifestation has begun). The next thing you know, you're nine months pregnant and asking yourself, what the hell did I do? That baby's going to come out where?

Yes, I'm joking about how babies are delivered, but to understand how and where things begin to manifest is important to when you'll see the pinnacles in your life begin to appear.

Having a baby is a step-by-step process after the thought has been manifested. It's the same with your business, it's a process.

After the first season of The Real Housewives of Orange County, I received so many emails from men and women wanting to know how they could do what I was doing — working from home. Donn saw the hundreds, if not thousands, of emails pouring in and quickly surmised that I needed a website, and more importantly, I needed to somehow capture all the email addresses.

As I replied to every email I could, I began to recall what I'd heard people say, "There are no coincidences." I sat quietly and found it very interesting that the manifestation of my previous thought could now possibly be bringing me an opportunity. I wasn't 100% sure what was actually happening, how everything would be tied together, but I knew just the same that there was a correlation.

Continuing to ask myself the right questions, I began to actually have some answers. I started looking for a place to move my business and even though I didn't last in that first office space, it was the first pinnacle toward expansion.

The next thing I know, I'm doing business with a company that wants to offer an on-line insurance course. How could I refuse? It seemed the universe had sent me thousands of people asking how they could do what I do and then the next knock on my door is someone who will help fulfill this segment of the manifestation.

I got my website up and running and could now offer an on-line insurance course. People began signing up, purchasing the workbook and taking the proper steps toward certification. The next thing you know … Bing! Bang! Boom! Pinnacle!

I took out a small business line-of-credit and moved into my own office. I decorated it exactly as I envisioned and the business now has room to grow. Soon, through my on-line site, Coto Insurance was up to 100 agents. Can you say Pinnacle? Then 200… Pinnacle! 300 … Pinnacle! 400 … You see where this is going? Let your thoughts flow, and whatever you do, don't fight them.

Today we have roughly 700 agents across the country and though not all are actively selling on a daily basis, the opportunity is available for them should they decide to take action. As a matter of fact, I'm reaching toward my latest opportunity to create more growth in my business, which in turn, means more money for my agents.

I'm speaking weekly on my own radio program, KABC 790AM, offering information to help retirees make sound decisions on where they should invest their life savings. I educate people on how I can assist them with their retirement goals and insurance needs, but that's not the pinnacle.

I'm reaching toward a nation-wide audience and any agent that works with Coto Insurance will be given leads in their state as they come in from the show. I am hoping that all the inactive agents will see this as an opportunity and get motivated to perhaps reach their own pinnacle.

WYSIWYG (what you see is what you get)... almost literally! If you see yourself as a failure, then that's what you'll be. If you see yourself as a housewife, that too will be manifested. Mind you, becoming something doesn't always happen instantly. You must keep an open mind, be approachable and understand that when opportunity is knocking on your door, you need to answer.

While watching a TV show about property improvements, I found it interesting that a man standing outside of a home improvement center was offering his free services as a landscaper. The man was very pleasant with everyone and found that those he spoke with were there in search of a way to enhance their yards or gardens. He made them an offer to come over and inspect their yard so he could tell them what they needed.

Unfortunately, everyone refused. Finally, a woman didn't turn him down, and in return, she got her huge backyard completely re-landscaped and turned into an entertainment paradise. The cost to her — free!

It's obvious that she manifested her thoughts. She wanted a really nice backyard, went in search of a way to make it happen, and sure enough, she opened the door when opportunity knocked.

Calling her husband and kids who were waiting at

home, she surprised them with the great news. When all was said and done, a few thousand dollars had been spent by the man that made the offer. Listen to what you want in life and then let it happen. Don't block the flow.

There are thousands of stories like this each and every day. Someone, at any given moment in time, is thinking of what they desire and letting the manifestation process begin.

What is your desire? How can you align yourself to it? Do you recall in the earlier chapter how you moved from one seat to another and I said that this was drive? Even in its smallest form? If you want to get technical regarding pinnacles, they, too, start from your drive being in alignment with desire.

Pinnacles are like milestones that we use to jump from one height to the next. If you want to climb Mount Everest you can't get there without first climbing up and down the smaller mountains that surround it.

A pinnacle, defined in the dictionary is a lofty peak. Do you have lofty ideas? Create the thought and do what it takes to reach that next peak ... manifest it. It really is as simple as this.

Training your mind to make changes and move beyond your comfort zone is a pinnacle in itself. I know I make it seem like pinnacles are just mind over matter, but really, that's all anything is when it comes to testing our self-imposed limits.

So, how do you align yourself with desire? Should I tell you? I think I already did. When you sit and think of what you want ... you're aligning yourself. When you ask the right questions, "How can I do this?" "What should I do?" then you've begun the process. When your desires are in alignment with your life's purpose, you will think the heavens opened up and showered you with every possible advantage. I'm living proof.

A great thing about reaching a pinnacle is when you know what your levels of attainment will be. You can actually chart the manifestations on a stat sheet and watch your desires appear. Everything is connected? Life is kind of like a game of business; how you strategize will determine whether you reach the pinnacles.

Are pinnacles just another way of saying that one has a goal to reach? Are pinnacles milestones?

Goals don't necessarily have to be in alignment with your purpose. It helps if they are, but one can have a goal to finish 1st place in a 10k race and it may have nothing to do with their purpose in life. A pinnacle is a level higher of where one is at present. Being your absolute best has everything to do with reaching newer, higher levels and also with being in alignment with one's purpose.

If you get a moment, stop what you're doing and take a pen and blank sheet of paper. Think back to the beginning of your life. You're in your crib and you may have just woke from your nap. Now, begin to list the pinnacles/ milestones throughout your life.

(Defined)
Milestone: A significant point in development.
Pinnacles: A lofty peak; Acme
Acme: The highest point.

It's important to understand that everything throughout your life is in development and though what I have listed as Pinnacles are also considered Milestones, it's my belief that neither is guaranteed. Both, pinnacles and milestones can be moment to moment or over long periods of time. Simply, they are just a higher point than one has previously experienced through actual personal achievement.

As an example:

Pinnacles/Milestones:
    Learned to crawl
    Learned to stand
    Learned to walk

> Learned crying brings company
> Learned to be potty trained
> Learned to reach for things to grab
> Learned to read
> Learned to ...

"Every successful person was once a beginner."
Everyone has set a goal, if only in their mind, and reached
the pinnacle in direct alignment with desire.

Some might take these bullet points as ridiculous or
consider them as just a part of life, milestones. The truth
behind each action is that you were aware of what you
wanted and you weren't afraid to reach for it, though it was
never guaranteed.

Continue making a personal list of pinnacles you
may have reached. There are many things you won't list,
taking some for granted as though you had no choice in
that activity. Your pinnacle list may not look like this, but
go ahead and make your own.

> Pinnacles/Milestones:
> Graduated high school
> Graduated college/trade school
> Joined the workforce
> Rented first apartment
> Created a saving towards buying a home
> Met/married spouse
> Purchased first home
> Had children
> Started my own business/landed great job
> Became a grandparent
> Gained recognition
> Retired

You've chosen to reach for any or all of these. The list
goes on, but the point being made, regardless of age or experience, you couldn't have reached one of these without a

personal desire. Each one is a point in development, a lofty peak reached and the newest high point of the moment.

If you could take all the pinnacles you've reached for in your life and pile them on the living room floor, how would they look? Would it be a sparse pile you could easily walk through or one that required a lot of maneuvering to get around and over?

I wouldn't say you've never achieved anything. In fact, every birthday in your life is a pinnacle. If you open your mind to all of your successes, large and small, you'll begin to see that much of what you saw as possible, actually happened.

You can start your own business more easily today, thanks to the Internet, which has opened up many avenues for success that didn't exist when I started in insurance. Whatever industry interests you, the Internet offers amazing opportunities without a big investment. If you can think it, you can do it.

See what others are doing. Offer something uniquely yours — whether it's your service, experience or quality product. Just because others may have been there before you doesn't mean you can't surpass them at the same game.

There were many companies on the Internet before Coto Insurance, but I built my own brand and carved out my niche. I brought in the right people, executed my business plan and reached new pinnacles.

I hope you took a moment to write down your pinnacles. There are so many people who won't acknowledge themselves. You owe it to yourself, your family and friends. It's important to realize you've done some incredible living, you're not just marking time. Before you reach your next pinnacle, be proud of what you've already achieved.

Think back about everything you've read regarding my life and you'll start to understand that we're in the same boat. I'm no different than you. In each and every chapter there is achievement and failure.

Included in every stat there are increments and

plateaus. The plateaus are where you'll find that you either reached a pinnacle or you're just a step short of it. At this point, do you give up or get busy? The answer lies in your personality. If you're used to giving up, then just this once, break through this programmed response. Change the program, rethink how you deal with disappointment and frustration. Take a new approach. Often the biggest obstacles to success are self-generated.

With each pinnacle you reach, stand back and admire your achievement. Enjoy the view from the top. Reward yourself for the hard work you've done. Keep setting shortrange goals that become the pinnacles of your business. Find the strength to lead when others want you to follow. And as you lead, handsomely reward those who helped you reach your pinnacles.

I heard a story of a businessman who shared a bottle of champagne with his executives for each pinnacle they reached. He kept the cork from each bottle and pinned a tag to it that kept track of the exact celebrated pinnacle. When he passed away, the staffer clearing out his desk, found over 500 corks dating back more than 50 years.

I wish I knew the entire history of this man and the company he created, but the message to me is clear: celebrate the pinnacles with the people who helped get you there. Keepsakes are relevant and remind us from where we've come — the muddy roads traveled.

Take the ideas that drive you and offer them to the world. Open yourself to every possibility, every opportunity. Don't fight it, flow with it. Set your sights on your next pinnacle.

Remember, pinnacles are the manifestations of thoughts in direct alignment with desires.

Chapter Nine

OC Housewives

The "Real" Show,
7-10 Minutes or Less

A good man by the name of Scott Dunlap who lives in Coto de Caza had always dreamed of producing a TV show about the privileged kids who lived behind the gates of this community. There was a casting call for these children, mostly college kids that were going away and then coming back home.

My son, Michael, wrote to the casting company executives letting them know he wanted to talk about his privileged life. He told them he lived in Coto de Caza when he wasn't in school at the University of Colorado in Boulder. When he's home during school breaks he's privy to a beautiful home, a great bedroom and dinner on the table every night, truly a very relaxing life of leisure.

He went on to inform them that his mother owns an insurance company, and works out of their house. He added that I was the only mom he knew who worked.

Well, NBC or Scott Dunlap got this letter and couldn't believe there was a woman behind the gates of Coto de Caza who worked. They came over to my house to speak with Michael, but he was back at college. They asked if they could talk to me and then informed me of the letter my son had written.

They asked if I played golf, tennis, or racquetball. I

just shook my head and replied, "There's no time for chasing balls here; I'm working ten hours a day." They questioned me and said, "You're not holding the fort down here." I told them that I was the breadwinner and my husband was okay with that. We have joint accounts that we put money into and it goes out the other end just as quick.

They questioned where I was from, inferring that I obviously couldn't be from California, because women here don't know how to work hard (their words, not mine). This led to their filming a short clip of me and taking it back to their studios. Bing! Bang! Boom! We got picked up. They began acquiring the other ladies for the show. They had my story and wanted to bring in four other ladies who didn't work. That's when the show became The Real Housewives of Orange County instead of the kids' show, Behind the Gates.

Scott, with his new vision, found that there truly were some hard-working women behind the gates. He thought most of the women just dabbled in jobs, played at charities, and couldn't really be the breadwinners. Being friends with Jeana Keough, Scott brought her on as an original member. One by one the housewives cast was coming together.

Laurie was working for me from my home office and that's where Scott met her. Scott, having produced plays, wanted this show to happen, so he took the whole concept to Bravo, who bought it. Talk about manifestations of thought.

There wasn't a big turnout for the casting call because no one really cared to do the show. My mother and quite a few neighbors thought I was nuts. I never really put much thought into the show. I figured we'd do something fun, and never imagined it would sell, that we'd actually be on TV. Here we are, five seasons later, and though the cast has changed, people across the country are still interested in the stories.

The first season, the producers and the crew just

showed up at the house. I wasn't prepared with anything. My hair was a mess and I wasn't wearing any make-up. I asked them what they wanted me to do and their reply was basically to just do what I normally did. Okay, I thought, but you're going to get really bored really fast.

It's difficult to grasp the concept that a reality show made up of cackling women would find a big audience and become a hit. The first season featured five hand-picked housewives, none of whom realized that they were a part of something explosive. With the start of the second season, we were called back amid a lot more buzz.

Many OC housewives saw how popular the show was, and how successful. They were beginning to see the upside of the Housewives fame.

The producers had their guideline of what they were looking for in women for the show. Many didn't measure up for a variety of reasons; didn't do well in front of the camera, not enough money, didn't exude enough drama. The show needed the WOW factor; it needed drama to keep viewers hooked.

If we were just Suzy homemakers, sewing, cooking and raising kids until our husbands came home, then we too would make pretty boring TV. We had to jazz it up, make it lively and fun to watch.

The show needed people that were eccentric in one way or another. If you were a big spender, worked too much, or had kids that ran your life, then you were a potential candidate for the show. When women didn't last more than a season, it was because they didn't stir the pot. They really didn't have or want any drama in their lives.

Tammy Knickerbocker was the classic example of a woman who flowed with her life. If things didn't go well, she dealt with it in a calm manner. This was great for her, bad for the show.

Significance was key and I was on Housewives because I was a working woman. I hadn't been handed my lifestyle. Everything I had, all the beautiful things, had been earned by my own blood, sweat and tears.

As for the drama part, I've had my share. Actually, before any filming begins for the day, the producers want to know what's happening in your life, what they're really looking for is a trigger that can be used to set an emotional hook for the audience. The more emotions, the better the ratings! Welcome to American reality TV!

Andy Warhol said we all get 15 minutes of fame in our lives. Well, the roughly 7-10 minutes of me you see in each show, in my view, is a ridiculous portrayal of who I really am. Most of my day is spent in my office, 10-15 hours. I'm either on the phone with a client, catching up on paperwork, answering important e-mails, dealing with my office staff or a gazillion other things that go much longer than a seven-minute reel.

My part of the show is often shot on the weekend. My business doesn't allow me to be in the gym between the 10 a.m. and 2 p.m. That's for women who don't work. All I can really say about this scenario is that I hope these women are covered in case of catastrophe. If their bread-winning husbands lose their jobs or leave them, they'd better have a back-up plan. This actually happened to one of the housewives, as I'm sure you've read. I'm a firm believer that everyone, men and women, must and should be able to take care of themselves.

People often ask me why I do the show. It started out as something fun, and in some respect, it still is. Yes, there is drama and dysfunction on the show which usually leads to someone crying on the way home, but at the same time, the rest of the show, when I'm not in frame, doesn't show the normalcy of my life, the day-to-day things that people have never seen me do — cooking a five-hour meal for family and friends, grocery shopping, getting the car washed, or even decorating the Christmas tree. The Housewives audience sees me involved in drama after drama. They must think this is all my life is about.

Though there have been a lot of heartfelt tears and

many moments of embarrassment, there have also been many good things to come out of this experience. My business has really boomed. I didn't even have a website when the show debuted. Another good thing happened when I was watching one of the episodes, I truly got to see and understand how mean I could be to Donn. He didn't deserve what I was dishing out. I really took to heart what I saw and vowed to work harder on our relationship. Because of the show, I've gotten to see parts of myself I don't like. Though I probably can't resolve everything I think might be an issue, I can put more effort into what means the most — my marriage.

Donn and I take time to discuss whether to be a part of another season. We've both agreed that if things get too far out of whack, we'll put family first and not renew our contract. Right now, the rewards to be on the show outweigh the negative impact. The opportunity to write this book, to appear on Jay Leno or Dr. Phil or in any of the magazines — it's fun and it certainly helps my business.

The cameras are always rolling. Drama seems to come out of nowhere. There was an incident in Las Vegas, where some guy came over, said I was beautiful and asked me to dance with him. While we danced, I told him not to sign the release the show's producers would hand him. The show can't air any segment involving the public without a signed release. When he walked out of the nightclub, he was pursued for his signature. I caught up with him and reminded him that he didn't have to sign a release. He instantly signed it anyway.

I just stared at the producers. They probably set up this whole thing. I instantly worked on figuring out the whole dynamics of the situation. Why did this guy come into the dance club, come over to me and ask me to dance and then leave in such a hurry? Why did he sign the release without reservation? I was very suspicious — staged reality, what a concept!

I had what I thought to be the answer to my looming

questions. Who signs a legal document without knowing what they're really signing? The answer — someone with intentions!

I immediately called Donn and told him that in six months he was going to see some guy twirling me around on the dance floor followed by a little kiss goodbye. I wanted Donn to be aware of this incident because I was sure the producers would try to make this into something bigger than it was. My husband understood, told me he believed me and encouraged me to forget about it and have a good time.

The interesting thing about this whole "reality" show concept is that the producers and people behind the camera are supposed to just film what's really happening, but they often provoke, edit and spin the shoot ... I've often wondered how many times the cast member of other shows have gotten in arguments with their producers about presenting them in a way that isn't real at all. Perhaps someone should secretly shoot the reality behind the "reality."

The relationships among the housewives on the show have been basically good. There have been some rough patches over the years, but for the most part, we do eventually resolve our differences. It's never an overnight ordeal, but slowly and surely, we gravitate back into each other's lives and realize our own shortcomings.

Some friendships fall by the wayside, such as the one with Laurie. She used to work in my home office, and though we were close, she eventually got married and we haven't really spoken since. She's living a beautiful life and I'm happy for her. Life goes on and people find other things they must attend to. Our friendship is not over, but seems to be on hold.

Of the cast members that I didn't particularly get along with, I would have to say that Jo and I aren't very compatible. Maybe it was the age difference or the fact that our priorities are miles apart. She seemed to be a know-it-all and I found it difficult during filming to be around her.

Men have asked me about Jo's irritating opening line, "And I deserve it." As one guy put it, "Yeah, she's cute, but what the hell does she do that she deserves anything? Deserves what, all the comforts of life because she has a cute face and ass?"

This kind of comment leads me back to my suggesting that women enable themselves, add to their own value and not look to a man for support. I'm not anti-men by any means; I'm just a realist. One day we all get old and we know what gravity is capable of doing. Men leave women all the time for a newer model. Depend on yourself not your man for your financial needs. Yes, one day we will all get old and wrinkly no matter how much Botox is available in the world.

The cast member personalities are only one dynamic; what's happening is another. As I think back on some of the most memorable shows I like or dislike, I think my favorite episodes are those where I'm having fun. I really like the time I showed up at Michael's college. I brought chips & dip to party with him and all of his friends. I took a risk showing up unannounced, but to me it was a blast! It was a little sad at first because it was such a surprise to Michael and could have led to a much more embarrassing situation for the both of us.

I enjoyed the episodes where I was with Briana shopping for her nursing uniforms. She had just been a senior in high school when the show started and now she's a college graduate with a nursing degree. It may not have made for the most exciting TV, but it's recorded and available for me to get sentimental over. My little girl was all grown up and doing great things with her life.

Obviously, the shows I dislike the most are the episodes in which I hurt someone's feelings. I've hurt Donn on more than one occasion. Not to justify my actions here in this book, but there were things he'd say that pissed me off. Then I'd respond in kind and only my end of the conversation would be caught on camera. The next thing I know, people are suggesting that Donn leave me.

The truth of the matter is that I still have a lot of growing to do. I have this saying that I believe in, "Hurt people hurt others." If you hurt me, I'm going to try to hurt you — not physically but verbally.

I now understand that when someone pulls the trigger, takes a verbal shot at me, that I instantly load my own weapon, my mind and then my mouth, with an explosive verbal assault. Though you won't know this by any of the seasons aired, I have worked on this issue. Sometimes I do get caught up in the negativity and it is tough to break away, go to a neutral corner and calm myself down.

One of the more exciting episodes to me was when Donn, the kids and I went Puerto Vallarta and got to experience zip-lining. It was so much fun. I love traveling and being adventurous with my family. It's the greatest time I could have. I think these trips take me back to the days of summer travel with my parents and siblings.

One scene really drew a lot of viewer comments. I drank Tequila with Briana who was 18 at the time. We did our one shot of Moonshine Tequila at a local restaurant that we know of in the village. It was fun and something we'll never forget. We were in Mexico where Briana was legally old enough to drink. It was a ceremonial toast with family; one time, one shot. By all the comments I received one would have thought that I was getting her drunk and giving her keys to a car. She wasn't being reckless with her life, and neither was I.

My kids had never been allowed to drink alcohol at home, nor had I ever bought them any alcohol while they were growing up. Though many parents think this is okay to do, I don't. I found some of the negative viewer comments out of line. I've never really spoken out about it before now, but I also don't believe it's my place to police other people or their kids.

There are times in "reality" TV when I'm sure the public realizes that there's a set-up to a scene like an argument between two cast members. No, it's not scripted, but if the producers find out that there is any kind of friction between cast members, they want to exploit it to the nth degree and that's their right. After the fight is over, when it comes time for each member to be alone on film and analyze her part in what happened, the public isn't privy to the director's questions and just sees the cast member venting aloud.

The question from the director or producer hits the editing-room floor and is replaced by background music or oftentimes, crickets — complete silence. This is when the viewer can be judge and criticize what the cast member thinks. It appears that the cast member just felt compelled to spill her guts on everything that took place. This is the real power behind reality TV. Unfortunately, it seems to patronize viewers and makes cast members appear insane, or just plain unstable. This is showbiz! Cha, Cha, Cha!

Oftentimes the women on the show are depicted as bitches — me more so than others. I've seen a lot of hateful reviews on the Bravo blog. When I do see these faceless, negative comments I revert back to the thought, "Hurt people hurt others." I wonder what's happening in the viewers' lives that make them want to insult others. A friend of mine says, "You accuse others of what you're most guilty of." Hmm, does this mean when people call me a bitch that they may be one too?

It makes me wonder why viewers who see me for all of 7-10 minutes an episode are so caught up in a program that exploits disagreements and often ignore resolutions to issues. Viewers don't get to see Donn and me go for a walk, or at home alone quietly enjoying each other's company. When looking at reality TV from the shooting side of the camera, I start to understand that Ozzie and Harriet would be laughed off the planet if they tried to do their show today.

No one wants to be classified or typecast as a "bitch," but to be honest, if someone wants to bring out the bitch in me, go for it! I'm not proud of this side of me; I'm just saying that no one is going to walk all over me. I've been through the wringer enough times where I'm not going to just sit idly by.

There truly is no reason to ever be a bitch. I appreciate most everyone I come across and oftentimes I go out of my way to accommodate others and make sure they're treated fairly. Whether I'm being served in a restaurant, dealing with staff, or working with a client, I make every effort to extend courtesy and understanding. In return, I expect a certain level of professionalism.

I think that the women on the show are considered bitches because they're assertive and argue with one another, but if these were men arguing, they'd simply be seen as aggressive. Apparently, any woman in the world that shows the emotion of anger is somehow instantly labeled as a bitch by someone.

It's definitely hard to watch myself on TV after it's all been filmed. I have a different perception of what happened in a given scene than what winds up on the tube. I believe people like to watch the show because train wrecks are mesmerizing. What's going to happen next? How could they do this or that? What are they thinking? I sometimes wonder if viewers are actually living vicariously through the cast and perhaps trying to figure out how they would handle a certain situation, like an argument with a friend. How the Housewives handle something may provide an answer for others in the "real" world.

If "OC Housewives" had to go toe-to-toe with Jerry Springer during ratings week, I think we'd win, hands down. It seems the drama has been getting juicier each season and the squabbles have become deeper and more intrusive than the arguments of the past.

Doing a show like this, I really needed to develop thick skin. There's a lot of hurt that is being dished out. Sometimes I wonder why I stay signed up for the craziness. There's a definite learning curve to expressing yourself season by season. Even though the producers want you to lay it all on the line, you quickly realize that there's a limit.

Perhaps, the learning is the "reality" part of the show. After Briana had split up with her boyfriend, Colby, she had to relive it when she saw them together on the final cut of the previous season, six months after the fact.

For a show that began on a whim and was originally intended to go in a different direction, it has become so popular that today we are seen in 72 countries. I receive e-mails from as far away as Australia and Japan. Never in a million years would I have thought it would reach the distance or cultures it has.

I'm not sure the show represents the American women in this country — not by a long shot. I believe there are valuable lessons that can be learned regarding humility and complacency. I wonder how a show would be developed in countries like China, Korea or Japan where the cultures are so much different.

Viewers try to pigeonhole the Housewives franchise. I've heard many comments, but I'll share one, "Same show, different town." Honestly, it's not the same show and even though each program deals with women and money, the personalities and situations are very different.

You can always find a similarity between two people who don't know each other and I've been compared to Jill from New York because she's a go-getter and doesn't take B.S. from anyone. I've also been told that New Jersey Housewife, Caroline, and I share similarities. I'll take that as a compliment, because I've met her once and she's really a nice person. Same show, different town? I concede, perhaps a little.

If there were anything I would like to have changed during the show's rise to fame would be to have had a higher awareness level of where the show was going and how I could have set a better example for the viewers.

Opportunity was knocking and I wasn't ready. I have made up for some lost time, but to be the example — I could have planned much better.

Though I don't consider myself a big celebrity, I can understand the divorce rate in the entertainment industry. The hours it takes to put a TV show together puts a tremendous strain on personal relationships and the limited time you have to spend with family. There's a lot of vulnerability in the industry and I'm sure some of the A-list actors we all read about experience thoughts such as … "Why should I stay, they're just weighing me down," or, "I'm the breadwinner, I can do what I want." I think that's a bit selfish. Everyone is usually fine in their relationships before they start doing a show, so what happens? As I've learned, balance gets betrayed.

Summing up the reality of this show, I've had a lot of good times, mixed with trying and difficult times. I truly recognize the fact that I've grown stronger as a woman. If this were all I took with me when the show is over, then I've really been blessed and that's the "reality" I've been looking for.

Chapter Ten

Out on the Town

What People Expect

I find it strange when I'm asked to sign an autograph. I'm not Angelina Jolie or Meryl Streep — I'm a reality star. In truth, I'm not even sure the word star is appropriate. I often find myself laughing inside when I'm approached. Then, when the moment is over and I've had time to reflect, it seems like I fall into a slight daze, "Did that just happen? Did someone really ask me for an autograph?"

It's not that we're the most popular women on TV when you consider all the soap operas and captivating shows available, but there are moments we can tell when someone has recognized us. People tend to be pleasant and very polite when asking for an autograph, though, there've been a few blushing moments when I've been asked to take a Sharpie to a bare chest. I usually oblige by drawing a big heart with the words — Love Vicki. God help them if they have wives at home.

A few years ago I was just another woman shopping in the local grocery store and didn't really notice a stare or second glance. Now it's really noticeable. I guess I can be thankful that my ethics are in, and the staring others do isn't for all the wrong reasons.

Oftentimes, when approached in a store or other venue, people offer respectable comments such as, "I like your work ethic." "I hope you and Donn make it." "You seem like a great mother."

Other people have the idea that because of the show, they know everything about me. I find myself biting my lip as they speak what's on their mind. I'm not going to change them, and until they hang out with me 24/7, they'll never really know me.

It's okay that people judge me. Everybody judges, day in and day out. As I've learned and will talk more about in the last section of the book, judgments are the way we call the shots moment by moment.

Most of the experiences I've had while out in public have been great. A few negative comments here and there are to be expected. I'd rather focus on the people who are just curious or have a general interest about the whole process called celebrity.

Being out on the town has become a well-planned event. I may be sitting at lunch with Tamra or another friend and suddenly the waiter is bringing drinks we didn't order. The male fans of the show know what each woman drinks and they don't hesitate to provide. This often leads to a few moments of chitchat, but never an exchange of numbers. That would be wrong, and thus far, I don't recall it ever happening.

After the ordeal with the producers and the man in Vegas, I learned to be very careful who is allowed into my circle. I'm still suspicious of the whole incident and probably always will be. My first thoughts are no longer about a friendly approaching fan, but more so, who is this coming and what's their angle? It's unfortunate that it has to be this way, but it seems that many people want to be on TV, and they don't care how it happens.

In one occasion, I received a threat of a lawsuit from a person I was dealing with who wanted to be on the show to promote their business. Luckily, I followed my gut on that particular situation and didn't end up doing business with them. God up above must have been looking after me.

The threat went away and my business deal moved forward with a more ethical company.

There have been a few uncomfortable moments when you don't want to be pushed or pulled. A person may want you for a photo-op or an autograph, but your mind is elsewhere, dealing with something that requires personal attention. Though I may not want to be asked to do something, I try not to deny the person asking; they don't know if I'm in the middle of a quandary. They're just doing what they do and truly are the epitome of a fan. It took me a few times to realize the entity called "celebrity."

I find it interesting that when I'm in a town far from home, usually during a business convention, people will approach me and ask where the rest of the cast is. They'll see me with a bunch of businessmen during a meal or strolling through a hotel lobby, heading for a conference room, and they don't always understand that the show is really just a small part of my life. It's a very integral part, but just the same, it's not my bread and butter.

One of my favorite moments on the town was when I surprised Michael during a frat party before a Colorado game. I arrived completely unannounced and Michael's friends were shocked to see me accompanied by the crew members with cameras. Michael was thoroughly embarrassed and it was an uneasy moment for the both of us. It was 10:00 a.m. and the beer was already flowing. Not one kid in the room hesitated to sign a release form. It turned out to be a lot of fun. I brought chips and dips and also stocked the fridge full of burgers, steaks and chicken. I even went so far as to buy the guys a cool grill. Everyone seemed to be okay with me being there, again, except for Michael.

Later that day, I spoke with Michael in private, letting him know that it was okay to be embarrassed and one day, if he does it right, he'll embarrass his kids. It's almost like a right of passage that one must bear through — their friends witnessing the crazy mom's actions firsthand. I figured that since I paid for Michael's college education, I could declare this as my God-given right, and take the liberty of enjoying at least one day of it.

When I reflect on that day, I know exactly how Michael felt. It was a different time, much different circumstances, but when I was young I ushered my friends through the house in rapid speed to avoid the embarrassment I would surely feel if they heard my mother ranting.

One day, when Michael is old and gray, perhaps recalling his college days, he'll smile and know how small of an incident it really was on the scale of things to be embarrassed about.

I've never really had anyone be brutally unfriendly toward me while out in public, but when it comes to the Internet, it seems there are some really mean people who hide behind pseudo screen-names and work at being hurtful. They say things like, "you're fat, you're ugly, you bitch too much, you're mean to Donn and you don't deserve him, you shouldn't do this, you shouldn't do that." They go on to pick at body parts or resort to nasty name calling. It's not only aimed at me. All of the girls on the show get this. It makes me wonder why these faceless people are hurling all these accusations. Are they feeling this way about themselves?

I'd really like to call these people out and say, "Let me see how you raise your kids. Let me see your nose. How heavy are you? Why are you so mean to people you don't even know?" Really, what in their life makes them so perfect? Truth of the matter, I don't believe they'll ever ask themselves pertinent questions such as these. They'll remain miserable in their skin while trying to project their hurt onto others. Oh well! Life goes on!

When I meet people while on the town and they make small comments or have opinions regarding something they saw on the show, I will earnestly listen. They may have a legitimate concern they want to share, but once again, they don't know if their concerns have already been dealt with. As an example: A woman told me that I don't respect Donn and I put him down too often. Though she may be right from her observation of the show, what she didn't see was Donn triggering me. The viewers will never see when things are resolved, because making up after a fight isn't good TV. The show promotes conflict and controversy.

I'm also often approached by young adults. They tend to gravitate toward me and I'm not sure exactly why, but possibly, they don't see me in the same category as their parents. Even though I'm probably the same age as their folks, I think they see how I've dealt with my kids, and quite possibly wish they'd had the same disciplines or guidance (just not the embarrassments). Truthfully, I don't question the attraction, but I do like having a connection with the younger crowd.

Some of the funniest times on the town are the woo-hoo moments. I somehow became the woo-hoo girl with my glass raised in the air, declaring, "Let's party! Woo-hoo!" I'll walk through a restaurant and while passing the bar a person woo-hoos me. I love it! I've been in my car when some college kids pull up next to me at a light. I know it's coming, so I wait for it, wait for it ...Woo-hoo! There it is. The light turns green and they're gone. I'm left in amazement with a smile on my face.

I received a birthday video from some fans that ran around town declaring to anyone they met, "It's Vicki's birthday. We need your best woo-hoo." It was filmed at Mc-Donalds, Starbucks and other establishments and people gave their best woo-hoo, even though you could tell they didn't have a clue as to who I am or what the shout-out referred to. The video was loaded onto YouTube, and to me, it was the coolest thing. It really does make you feel special when people you don't know are thinking about you and having fun with something you did. It just goes to show, if you do something enough times, eventually it catches on and make its way into society.

Though I don't expect the show to last for many more seasons, I'm anticipating a change in the recognition factor when I'm out on the town. By releasing this book and building my business bigger, I will once again, "break away" into a new reality. This time I would prefer it to be about the challenges of life and helping others break through to new realms.

Who knows, perhaps I could do a show that inspires men and women to break barriers and step beyond their normal day-to-day routines. Wouldn't that be cool?

So, the expectations when out on the town have been readily accepted as part and parcel of the whole "reality" experience. If the day comes that it's unbearable, I'll just shake my head and ask myself, "What the hell was I thinking?" Truly, though, I don't believe that day will come since I tend to absorb what's happening, get in a major wrestling match with it, and once again, whether I like it or not, face the next experience.

In the next chapter, Social Media, I answer questions from fans that were posted on my Facebook fan-page. Then, in the last chapter of Section Three, "The Experience Overall," I will keep it short and sweet, such as the TV life of most reality stars.

Chapter Eleven

Social Media

Questions From Fans

How did the world exist without social media? We have so many ways of staying in contact, finding past friends or learning information that takes our daily lives to a new level of intelligence. Through the use of cell phones and texting capabilities, there is no longer a delay when one wants to share anything on their mind. With so many social media sites on the Internet, Twitter, Facebook, YouTube, MySpace, Blogspot and unmentioned others, if anyone wants to speak their mind or change the world by starting a movement, the opportunity in now available to do so.

In my office, I have someone that handles my viral marketing needs. About a month ago he posted a statement and a question on my Facebook and Twitter site, to the fans of the show. The statement was, "Vicki is writing a book." The question was, "If you could ask Vicki anything, what would you like to know?" We actually got a nice turnout of people with respectable questions. Then, we also got a few that had opinions or statements of their own. The first post is from a guy named Joe R. He doesn't really have a question, so perhaps he didn't understand what we were looking for.

We wanted this book to be inclusive of those who made the show what it is today, and yes, even Joe's thoughts are important to me. He gives me insight as to how I come across on the show. For that, thank you, Joe. Also, thanks to everyone that took the time to ask a question and participate in my book.

Though I will answer each question individually, you will find most of the questions have already been written about. This happened before we posted on the social sites.

Questions & Answers

Joe R. - I think it's annoying you all want to write a book. We watch you on reality TV show. We know your life. We know about you.

A- You may think it's annoying that some of the ladies are writing books. I think, because of what I know, I can share some great information with the masses. This information can help others to create a business that supports their family. You watch a reality show that shows you roughly 10 minutes of me. I live 24 hours a day and you think you know me through 10 minutes. Hmm. Who is living in reality?

Jill L. - Everything ... no actually, I would like to know how you tolerate Gretchen and Slade (just kidding).

A- Gretchen and I aren't the best of friends. I was in my teens when she was born. We're in two totally different worlds when it comes to our lives. As long as I remember this about her, I'm okay. As for Slade, again, we're not the best of friends.

Ashley S. - I would like to know, how did you know insurance would be your career?

A- I didn't always know. What I did know was that I liked the business aspect of it. Later, I realized that it was a big part of my purpose in life ... making sure others are looked after and are safe.

Gregory O. - I'd like to know how you're the only housewife of the OC, NYC, NJ, and ATL that has made her own money. I love it!

A- I don't know why, other than to say that I learned not to rely on others for my needs or wants. If you want something... go and get it!

Ashley S. - And how did you know you wanted to do the TV show?

A- I didn't know at first. I didn't really know exactly what to expect. No one ever said they were going to film a show that would depict controversy between women in a wealthy neighborhood.

John N. - The Million Dollar Question: How did I become a member of the million-dollar round table?"

A- I don't know. How did you become a member of the million-dollar round table? I presume you did something the garnered that. If you're asking me how I did it ... I worked for it. Plain and simple ... work, work, work.

Joey E. - Having an "A" Personality ... Is that what drives you to be so good in business? Or is it something you learned on your own through school? Natural or Taught?

A- I would have to say that I learned by watching my father. He was a very smart man that could multi-task with the best. We had nice things because he had the drive to get them. If you want something nice, you have to go toward it, not away from it. DRIVE!

Sabrina D. E.- I love you on the show, I like most watching

you interact with people and I love to hear you having fun! I do like to read books, so if you write one, I would be interested to learn more about what you do with your free time! How you have fun and why you do the things you do that make you so interesting. You are my favorite housewife!!!

A- Thank you, Sabrina. I enjoy many things when I have free time (which isn't too often), but I spend some quiet evenings with Donn, I take yoga classes, wine tasting, spa treatments and an assortment of other small venues. I travel for work a lot and wish I had more time to explore the towns I visit.

Pam-Rick D. - What drives you? You are a very successful businesswoman, why and how did you get there? That is what we want to know.

A- Pam- Rick, - I cover this in an earlier chapter, but really, I'm a success in business because I stay in the vibration of drive. When I want something, personal or business, I figure out the steps I need to take and start the drive. One of the mottos I like—> Go big or go home!

Katrina G. - Have you always had the confidence to be the person you are today? Have you ever struggled with your goals and how have you dealt with disappointments? I lack a lot of confidence in myself and would just love to take on life and goals the way you do.

A- Great question, Katrina. No, I haven't always been as confident as you see me. I had to mentally change my mind and stop listening to the part of me that doubted my abilities. I have had quite a few disappointments in my life, but have decided that I should use them to inspire myself. When I realize that I have lived through a disease that could have killed me, I had to ask myself, what else could I take on? What else has the world got to throw at me? Bring it on! You will only lack confidence if you choose to lack it. Stop listening to the negatives in your life and choose to push forward. If I can do it, I know anyone can ... including you.

Kiah C. - I'd like to know the process for being chosen for Real Housewives of the OC.

A- The Real Housewives of Orange County actually started with the idea of a show regarding college kids living a privileged life in Coto de Caza. It turned into what you see now because they found that there was a woman behind the gates at Coto that actually worked for a living ... me.

Dan Z. - Thank you miss Rachel!! Lol. I think in times like this that so many Americans are losing their homes and jobs ... that people like to read about other people making it ... building themselves up ... if you're going to write a book ... at least make it worth it ... give someone hope in a new tomorrow. Especially coming from such a strong woman like Vicki ... it would mean a lot to many. If the book is based on that ... I will definitely be in line waiting to buy it.

A- Dan, that's exactly what this book is about. Helping others to understand that there is a way for them to create a better lifestyle or business. I even offer help in the last chapter for people that want to learn the process of becoming a life insurance agent, if that is the path they seek. I'm a firm believer that being self-employed is the way to go. Make life and business happen the way you want it to. I hope this helps you and others out there.

Rachel H. - I like Dan's idea above, Vicki! That's what I'd want to read about.

A- Then you shall. I hope you like the book. Let me know what you think.—Vicki G.

Jill L. - I want to know how you raised such a mature, responsible daughter like Briana? She's great!

A- Did she put you up to this? LOL. Briana is great and I am very proud to be her mother. I was a hands-on mom with both Mike and Briana. I didn't allow them to fail. They weren't allowed to have sleepovers at other people's houses, and I put them in private high school, which I think made a huge impact on their life. I also told them "college was not an option!"

Jessica M. - What about your past life? Who is the guy you talked about last season on the 1st episode, (B & Mike's Father) were you married to him? My reasoning would be because BEFORE being on ROCHW, you had a normal life, just like everyone else.. Not for people to say "OMGosh Vicki did this or Vicki did that" for the fact of saying "HEY, Everyone has a past & is entitled to a wonderful change!!!"

A- I was married to a man named Mike during my 20s. We divorced after nine years of marriage. Surprisingly to some, I don't have a crazy past. I have had some challenges that have made me who I am today, but other than people thinking they know me through the show, I am normal … whatever normal is, eh? I do have to say that all of my friends would tell you that I did have a crazy, busy life before the TV life. So, I guess in that regard, nothing has changed.

Kelly P. - I want to know about how you made all your $$$$ and the transition from being single mother to a fab business woman?

A- Purpose, drive and action. You may have read about these in Section Two of the book, "Business." It's really all about having goals and knocking down the roadblocks until you reach the pinnacles you set out to achieve. Do what you love and the money will follow ... Always chase an opportunity, NEVER a paycheck!

Amanda T. J. - How about 20 things we don't know about you ...

A- This is a tough one. I'm pretty much an open book. Just ask the first guy, Joe R. He seems to think he knows me. LOL. How about one thing for now? Though I like to go out and have fun, I'm still pretty conservative.

Caroline Anne C. - Why not write a HOW TO book: how to become successful and build an empire like you have done???

A- That's what we're doing. Won't you join us?

Bettina J. B. - I would like to know the top 10 things you would like to do before you are 60 years old...

A- 1) I would like to have an ocean view home. It doesn't have to be big, just an ocean view. 2) My goal by the time I'm 60 is to have enough money to retire comfortably. 3) My goal is to have my primary residence paid for with no mortgage. 4) My goal is to live near my sister and brother. 5) My goal is to spend at least 2 months a year in Puerto Vallarta at my condo. 6) By the time I'm 60, I'm hoping to be a grandmother. I want to teach my grandchildren how to sew and bake cookies. 7) I'd like to still have Coto Insurance, but only having to work a few days a week to make sure it is running smoothly. 8) I would like to invest my time with a charity of my choice. 9) I'd love to be able to take a walk on the beach every morning when I'm 60. 10) I want to be alive and healthy and happy and to have my entire family blessed by my hard work and dedication!

Brandy P. – I would like to know how you get to be so successful?

A- I got to be successful by taking one step at a time and also by not doubting myself. If I failed at something or made an error, I refocused and did things differently until I found what worked.

Ivy J. - Yay!! I would love to know why and how you never seem to let anything come in the way of you and your goals?

A- I focus on what I want. I push forward quickly and work until I get to my goal. If something is supposed to take four months, I'm adamant about doing it in two.

Deena P.T. - What resources did you use to start your business? How much start up money did you need & where did you get it? What do you think are the BEST resources available for middle class people(without capital) to start a business? What were some of the bumps in the road you experienced on the way to success & how did you overcome them? What & Who...

A- Deena, what great questions. To start the life insurance selling business, you need a computer, a phone line and an Internet connection. I needed a credit card with NO balance on it so I could use it to charge for my leads. I had a $10,000 credit and every time I got paid on cases, I paid the credit card off right away. I never spent more than I earned and started saving money when I had a surplus. I think the best resources to start or own your own business are ones that are recession proof. I had a lot of bumps in the road and still do. It's never smooth sailing, but definitely not as rocky as it was at the beginning.

I overcame the bumps because I WANTED TO SUCCEED and failing was not an option for me because I had nothing else to fall back on.

Rick H. - The secrets of the OC Housewifes?

A- The secrets? Is someone keeping a secret? According to some viewers they know all, which means there are no secrets.

Andrew M. - Do you wax or shave???

A- I've had laser hair removal. No more waxing or shaving for me!

Peter V.S. B. - Talk about your religion.

A- I was baptized Lutheran and went to Sunday School every week. I was confirmed when I was in 8th grade and also joined Awanas, which was a church group. I was married to Donn at Willow Creek Church in Barrington, IL, and took 9 months of pre-marital classes before we were married.

We are currently members at Saddleback Community Church where Rick Warren is our pastor.

Andrew C. - Where do you get your ambition? What truly motivates you?

A- What motivates me is the feeling I get internally when I am successful. When I get an award for being the top agent in the country, when I'm told I am mentoring others across the country to change their lives — it's like someone lights a fire under me and there's no putting out the flame. It's a natural high, one that I love to feel. I'm not sure this has anything to do with it, but I'm an Aries, and when I talked with an astrologer long ago, he told me that the way the planets were lined up when I was born was pure "energy". I guess there's no stopping me no matter how hard people try.

Sara Y. - How did you get in the business that you're in?

A- A friend sold me a policy during my first marriage and I saw that she was able to make a good living as a single mother. Later, when I divorced, I asked her how I could do what she was doing.

Glenda L. - The balancing act of being a career woman, mom and wife.

A- The balancing is tough. Now that the kids are grown and have careers, the load is a little lighter, but still, the 15-hour workday, shooting the show on weekends, the business travel … it puts a strain on a family, but you have to keep the goals in mind and know that you're doing this for your family's security.

Holly N. - How you dealt with your move from Chicago to Ca? How you dealt with divorce? How you met Don? How you got so successful? Hardships and fun times at where you are now and how you decided and heard about real housewives?

A- Donn took a job in Southern California about 3 months prior to us getting married. Once we were married, I moved with the children to CA. We didn't know anyone and it was very difficult to figure out how to fit in. I didn't like CA for at least 2 years and wanted to move back to IL. I longed for my family and friends. It was a huge culture shock. A lot of things are different in the Mid-west, especially the fact that people actually know their neighbors. I dealt with the divorce by finding a career and deciding to make something of myself instead of depending on anyone else.

I first met Donn when I was in my early 20s and we worked

for the same company. He went away and then later, just as my divorce was about to be final, we happened to run across each other while I was out with a friend.

Hardships would have to be the divorce and seeing the kids hurt by their father's inability to be there for them. Fun times are the family outings, the traveling and river trips.

My son, Michael, wrote a letter that led the producers to my door. In the first chapter to this section of the book there are more details.

Sheila H. J. - To let your guard down and be relatable, for instance, talking about a fear you had as a young woman and how you overcame that fear. Also, I would recommend sharing your faith and how it carries you from one trial to the next. People watching you on TV don't get the whole picture. Take note of what is edited out of scenes you thought would make it to the airwaves and then share those moments as special photo comments in the middle of the book. Lots of personalities have done biographies that are highly entertaining and heartfelt, giving a history of themselves. Dolly Parton's book was one of those that I really enjoyed because she is very "real" and honest about how she feels.

A- I had so much fear as a young single woman with 2 kids that I would cry myself to sleep while praying to God that he would watch over me and to never leave me. I had a great support system with my girlfriends and family members. I never felt truly alone.

I think faith is a very personal and private matter. I do not publicly display my faith, as I don't want to be ridiculed or judged by anyone saying it doesn't fit the "mold" that they think I should fit in.

I overcame my fear, knowing that as long as I am healthy, have food on my table and a roof over my head – anything could be accomplished

Mel J. - I think it is really good to talk about how the competition in the market in the area of insurance made you work harder to secure big accounts to maintain your license and expand your business. Who was the driving force that gave you the drive to go and grab the big accounts and reach your targets? How has networking helped you and what is the secret in getting your clients not to go elsewhere for business but keep giving you their business.

A- I set goals every month and every year of what I need to make in order to pay my bills and to save for retirement. I do not quit until I reach those goals. I break them down by weekly goals, monthly and then annually. As long as those goals are set on paper I will never fail, because I stay focused and on course.

I'm a big believer in networking. I formed a networking group called LeTip here in Orange County and was voted the fastest growing LeTip group in the country.

Stephanie M. - You know, you are such a California Girl, and we forget that you actually grew up in the Midwest. Can you talk more about that ... was there any culture shock when you first moved to CA? What is the difference between the Midwest and CA? What aspects of you are Midwestern? I'd also like some of your insights on child-rearing. Why did your kids turn out so great? What made the difference?

A- There is definitely a HUGE difference between CA and the Midwest. I still have my Mid-western values and don't think they will ever leave. I see here in CA that girl friend-ships aren't as important as they are in the Mid-west.

Where I was raised, every night the garage door stayed open, we mowed our own lawns and we grilled dinner with our neighbors. Here in CA, when people return home from work they open their garage door, drive in and shut it right behind them. There is no social interacting with the neighbors the way we did back home.

I also think people in CA tend to live beyond their means. In IL, we are more conservative and humble and not as flamboyant.

To me child rearing is the biggest task we have. Our children are our future and if we do not raise them to be respectful and educated, our future will be compromised. I was very strict with my kids and never gave them a rope long enough to hang themselves. In return, I have great kids that respect me and what I have done to provide for them. It's an amazing reward.

Emelie M. - Everything! How were you as a teenager for example?

A- I was like every other teenager in the world. I was a bit self-absorbed, but had a lot of friends. I always enjoyed taking friends on vacations to our cabin on the lake in Hayward, WI. I was not athletic, but always in the popular crowd.

Jan M. - The lessons you learned, the blessings of prosperity in your life today, and sharing your gifts of love and laughter throughout the book?

A- I've learned so many lessons and unfortunately they've mostly been through the school of hard-knocks. I believe I'm prosperous because I'm on purpose. I want to see that people are safe and financially secure. I do love my family and friends and laugh as often as possible.

Ileen G. - From your beginning to now… what steps you took to get to where you are today with your business?

A- The steps are different for many businesses, but for me, the only way to explain them would be to say, "one foot in front of the other and having a clear focus in mind that I was going to be successful." Not "IF" I was going to be successful! As each day brings new problems, I work to resolve them as quickly as possible. Doing this enables me to continue moving forward without dragging excess baggage.

Mel J. - Vicki… your kids are lovely and somehow they have taken in your husband in a very positive way, how did that transition happen? Your husband is so sweet and nice, you are you and he doesn't stand in the way… do you think you can be with him and get closer to him now that the kids are off to college? Also, about Gretchen, she grows on the audience but she hasn't grown on you… are there conflicts between you two that we don't see in the episodes? Are we sending a negative message to our kids or the younger generation that if you marry a rich man… you can grab his wealth or further your own life and career?

A- Donn and my kids get along well now. It hasn't always been easy for any of them, but I think there is a mutual admiration and respect between them. Mike and Briana were 7 & 8 when Donn and I married. Back then, I think the kids would have rather seen me stay single. Now that they are adults, it is much easier on everyone and there is no longer any competition.

Gretchen and I are not the best of friends because she's 17 years younger and we have completely different lives.

As for sending negative messages to kids regarding women marrying men for their money… Most smart rich men will have an iron clad pre-nuptial contract. Let's not forget to mention, these wealthy men with young women know what they're getting into, or should I say, what they're buying. It takes two to tango. As one of my friends has always told me, "If you marry for money, you pay for every penny of it somehow"

Vicki F. F. - Hi Vicki...... I guess I would like to know what really drives you? You are just so darn driven!!!! God Bless! Vicki.

A- If I had to dig really deep, it might be fear; the fear of not being able to provide for my family. I'm also in fear for others and their family. I cringe when I hear of the death of a breadwinner leaving a spouse and three kids with no insurance to cover the mortgage or bills. It's sad and happens all too often. My goal is to insure and educate as many people as I can on the importance of life insurance and proper retirement planning. There is a 100% chance a person will die. My goal is to be sure they are covered with life insurance before they do.

Andrinique D. - Pretty Photo, cute dress!

A- Thank you, Andrinique.

Brenda T. - The back story of your life.

A- That is in the whole section regarding my childhood and young adult years.

Dean F. - I would love to learn more about your early days... when you worked at Jewel and the struggles of being a young Mom and how you rose from the ashes. I grew up in Kenosha and have family in Northern IL, so getting back to your roots would be very interesting to me. Hugs!

A- That too, is all in the section regarding my childhood and young adult years. I'm not sure about getting back to my roots, as I feel they are ingrained in me and I've never truly left them.

Lisa W.G. - I would like to know how you grew up. I would like to know your struggles, if you had any, becoming a successful career woman. I would like to know why you hold on to your independence so tightly, even though you seem to have everything you need in family life. There must be a reason and a past that made you so driven, that you just don't want to stop. It can't be all financial. I WOULD BUY THAT BOOK.

A- There are reasons why I am so driven and they are in this book. As mentioned before, it may have to do with the fear of not being able to support my family. I saw how devastating it was when my father lost everything due to an unscrupulous person.

Molly C. - What do you eat for breakfast??!!

A- I eat 2 eggs scrambled with spinach or a protein drink. NO CARBS for breakfast ... ever!

Michelle R. K. - High school/early marriage days, relationships with sibs, life when the kids were tots... why Vicki is who is she is today.

A- All of this covered in the section regarding my younger years. I am the way I am like you are the way you are. We take our experiences, internalize them and make decisions on how we think our lives should go.

Christine D. G. - what made you decide to move to CA. and how you met Don.

A- I met Donn a second time around, just as my divorce was finalizing. He had accepted a job in California, a place I had always dreamed of living. I sold my condo and together we put a down payment on our new home.

Christina S. - Your insecurities and divorce to your first husband? Interesting & helps other people deal with their own I guess?

A- When I asked my first husband if we should get divorced, he said "ok". It was actually not the answer I was looking for, but I went ahead and filed. My insecurity was my fear of being alone; not having a boyfriend or spouse to help me raise Michael and Briana. Though there were times when I was single that I wasn't really comfortable being alone, I kept thinking there was a bigger plan for me than what I was doing. I do want to clarify that I never got involved with anyone because of this and I believe one is not ready for a relationship until they are okay with not having a relationship. You have to be "ok" by yourself, before you can be "ok" with someone else.

Randy R. - How has the lack of anonymity affected you?

A- My business boomed. People saw what I was doing and they wanted to either get involved with Coto Insurance or learn what they could do to make a better living. Not being anonymous has put a lot of people to work, so I'm okay with giving up a little of my private time. I went from working by myself with1employee, to now having 8 full time employees and over 700 agents across the US, selling insurance under my system. Check out the final section of this book to learn more or go to cotoinsurance.com for more information on how, you too, can become licensed and work in this amazing career.

Joe D. - Where does your passion for success come from?

A- When a client passes away and everyone is walking in with cakes, flowers and dinners, I walk in with a check from the insurance company. I am able to reassure a bereaved mother of children that everything is going to be okay because her husband was responsible enough to buy life insurance. It's a feeling that cannot be explained and is the reason why, every day ... I am changing people's lives. It feels very good and is my purpose.

Chapter Twelve

The Experience

Overall

One could suggest that an experience such as this is rather vain. Well, whatever one thinks, just the same, I've enjoyed the heartfelt tears, the laughter, the anger and every other form of emotion that reminds me just how alive I am.

From a show that started with an idea about rich kids to five seasons that follow the dramatic affairs of privileged housewives, one just has to be amazed at the longevity — regardless if they like the show or not.

The show has helped my business flourish to a level I never could have imagined before Michael's letter and the first knock on my door that kicked it all off.

The second season proved to me that flukes do happen and can actually work out okay. By the third year, a few new cast members were on board and a few others were gone, which I found a bit difficult to deal with. Even though I wasn't the best of friends with Jo, she was a part of the whole and original group. I wasn't interested in the changes the producers were making; then again, who am I to tell them how to run a show, who to bring in and why.

With each new season and the prettier the girls involved, I've sometimes felt intimidated. I've cried my share of tears by hurtful accusations, but when I consider the source and what I have achieved in my life, I know not one of them can touch me.

They can't understand why I don't show up to the gym in the afternoon for a leisure four-hour workout. Some people have responsibilities and don't rely on others for a beautiful lifestyle. I don't spend the majority of my time trying to fit into the jeans of a teenager.

Through my business acumen and ethics, I'm creating a bankroll that could cuss out the meanest of sailors, let alone a pretty young thing that wouldn't know what to do if her spouse were to up and walk away.

Eventually, 30-year-old Gretchen, became the newest cast member. I was 17 years old when she was born. We're in two different worlds, yet we're under one roof of "reality." We'll never be in the same league for anything and the only reason I bring this up is because of the overall experience; the mixing of beauty, age and money that makes me step back and ponder my life.

The conclusions are obvious: one day, not even Botox will help reverse gravity, and if all I can depend on in this life is my looks, then I will have failed myself miserably. These are the types of things that doing the show has clarified for me.

As for my family from Chicago, my mother has expressed on numerous occasions that she doesn't like the show and the way I am. She believes I've become very vain and lost my Mid-western values since moving to California.

My sister Lisa, didn't like the show very much because it doesn't show the real Vicki. It showed someone that she didn't know and that made her sad.

As for my brother, Billy, he thinks it's a kick in the pants and throws beer parties when the show resumes from a seasonal break. On occasion, he'd been visiting during filming and was on a show or two. He once surmised that I was lucky to have had this experience for the past five years; it's something I'll look back on and understand its impact on my life.

Basically, the show has given me a legacy that my

great-grand kid will be able to see. If I can possibly embarrass a whole future generation, well, then maybe Michael will really shake his head, shrug his shoulders and say, "That's my mom. Woo-hoo and all!"

The experience of seeing my verbal assaults spewing forth really opened my eyes the most. There were times that Donn's co-workers had seen the show and he'd be at work defending things that I'd said. That had to be of great embarrassment for him and if there's anything I do regret in this life, it's when I speak without thinking of the consequences. I do feel that I should be a bigger person and apologize for my actions.

Though there have only been a couple of occasions where the paparazzi have taken any pictures, I laughingly figured they mistook me for some blonde bombshell that was bigger than life. The majority of pictures taken have been from fans and the crew. I will add that it was a surreal feeling when on a trip to the Vatican, I was greeted by people from Ireland, Australia, Poland and Greece that recognized me from the show. I've just really never been able to wrap my head around the idea of a little housewives show with a reach that spans the globe.

The show has had a huge effect on my business. When I think of all the agents I have across the country and the new ones coming on, my head just spins. The show has enabled me to create jobs for others and share an opportunity with those willing to take charge of their careers. While other companies are laying people off, we're increasing our staff and agents.

Then there are all the people that have become protected with life insurance and have taken the necessary steps to covering their family in the case of emergency or catastrophe. I don't know that this would be as huge as it is or as possible if it wasn't for the show.

When asked, "In what ways has the show really deeply changed me," I had to sit and think how to express myself.

I'm more sensitive and critical of myself when I see my image and personality on the TV. I know I've changed immensely, but still have my moments when I get overwhelmed and flustered. I see all of my faults and it can be embarrassing to have reached this age and not be totally calm about life. I'm aware of the inadequacies and while trying to cope with a hectic schedule each day, I know I need to find a moment to let some things go.

What tomorrow brings is anyone's guess. Would I like to do another show? I've thought about it, but it would have to be something different, lighter in venue and emotional tone. I don't believe everything has to be controversial to be successful.

When all is final, said and done, the show is over, the curtain has dropped and I've moved on, I'm sure I will be thankful for the experience and I know I will be continuing to find my center, to be at peace.

At this point, I would like to thank those of you that followed The Real Housewives of Orange County. I've truly loved the whole concept and everyone I've gotten to know, either personally or through my business, via this show. Whether you realize it or not, you've helped me to grow from within. It's been an incredible journey. Thank you from the bottom of my heart.

Section Four

My Thoughts

Chapter Thirteen

Personal Views

Foundations and Beliefs

Everybody has an opinion, a point of view. This includes me. I believe that every person or family needs a firm foundation, but in the 21st century, it's hard to have when the availability of certain products are so easy to acquire. Top that with the fact that marriages have an over 50% failure rate. I believe people, in general, have lost sight of what a foundation consists of.

Some would have you believe that if you don't have God or Jesus in your life, a personal savior, then you're lost and minus a foundation. I disagree. Though I do have my strong beliefs in God, I know many people that don't, yet they're some of the most ethical and morally responsible people I've ever met.

What this means is that minus a belief in any one religion, they have their personal checks and balances that they adhere to. I can appreciate these people, regardless of our differences of opinion about religious beliefs.

I've never once heard of someone in despair asking a fireman if he had accepted Christ as his personal savior before the despondent allowed himself to be rescued. The fireman would more than likely save a life, regardless of his job, because deep within he has a foundation or a belief that says human life is valuable.

Foundations exist because of one's belief and until

the belief is somehow changed, the structure built upon it remains sound for that person. Sometimes a person will change their belief and eventually find that their new way of life doesn't work so well. It's nice to know that one can always re-create their life as they see fit and return to previous beliefs.

It is my belief that though there are many good public schools available, I would rather have my children enrolled in a private or parochial education system.

One day, Donn and I were discussing Michael and Briana's future high school options. I decided to drive around town and take a really hard look at the local high schools.

I went to a public school and watched as all the kids were exiting for the day. It was roughly 1:30 in the afternoon, which to me, seemed like it was a bit early. I wondered where these kids would be going if their parents weren't done working for the day?

The next thing I noticed about the kids was the way they dressed; boobs were barely covered and baggy pants hanging lower than they were designed to be worn. I could actually see some of the kids lighting up cigarettes as they got into their cars. The immature actions I saw that day spoke volumes to me.

When I went to the Catholic school parking lot for observation, though we're not of this religion, I saw kids leaving the grounds in a very respectable manner. The girls were dressed appropriately in plaid skirts with white collared, neatly pressed tops while the boys were uniformed with belted khaki Docker slacks (not hanging low), white and blue golf-style shirts that were appropriately tucked in. To me, these kids seemed to be sharp, mature and very classy.

I've heard the argument that uniforms stifle a personality, but I disagree. Again, that goes back to opinion. I have this belief that uniforms are the way to go when it comes to a school setting. First and foremost, schools are for educating the mind, not a social venue to display what one does or doesn't have. Though the private schools seem expensive, I knew that by enrolling my kids in this type of system it was going to benefit them and their future.

If you'll notice, when a child goes off to a military type of school, they usually come back as very educated young adults. I think this truly supports the argument for uniforms in the education system and debunks any idea that a public school is less stifling. As a matter of fact, I'd wager that overall, public schools are more stifling and detrimental to a child's intelligence.

I believe the saying "Dress for success" holds true in this situation. When Michael and Briana left for school, they always looked prim, proper and mature. I felt extremely proud that I was giving them an education beyond the public system. I truly believe this set a firm foundation and prepared both of them for a successful college education.

I don't know if there is anything more important to building a strong foundation for today's youth than to give them a proper education and loving support from family.

Having a firm foundation is extremely important in a marriage. This solid foundation is often supported by strong personal and moral ethics. If one's foundation has cracked and a divorce is imminent, a new foundation can be created. Each adult should still accept the responsibility of having children and do everything possible to remain a supportive parent. This doesn't mean that one should just throw money to the ex-spouse and say, "You deal with it." It means going to the kids' sporting games and activities, being involved in their education and speaking to your ex as though they were still a friend (even if you don't like it).

If you act mature toward your ex-spouse when you're around your kids, then come the day, God forbid, that your grown kids should ever divorce, they'll be able to keep an open communication with their ex-spouse, which can only benefit their children.

So how does one build a strong foundation? Well, I

think the first thing to do is to examine what one believes. If you want to know what you truly believe in, write it down. Make a list of what you value in life. Make a list of why you value it. Are you firm on getting the best education possible? What do you think being married really entails and what should you do to make it last? Do you curse around your kids or your parents? If so, what is that teaching your kids and what does it say about the way you were raised? There are many things to contemplate while making a list of personal beliefs, but once the list is available, you'll have the opportunity to know yourself so much better than you do now.

I've met so many people who think that kids today are disrespectful. Well, these people may be right because many parents don't teach their kids to have respect for anyone, in or outside of the home. There's a reason one of the last generations was called the entitlement generation. Parents have stopped policing their kids. I'm not an advocate of hitting a child to correct a wrong, but it sure seemed to work effectively on my generation. "Go get me the belt," or, "Bring me the bar of soap," are almost completely lost commands. If you were to tell an unruly child either of those lines today, they'd look to see if your pants were falling down or your hands were dirty.

I believe it's important to teach children to have and understand what a strong foundation is. You can teach by example and through lecture. Why does Mommy get dressed up for work instead of wearing jeans and a t-shirt? Why does Daddy put on a clean uniform when it's just going to get dirty again? Why can't we watch TV during dinner? Focusing on little things brightens a child's mind just as much as bigger issues. As the song says, "I believe the children are our future; teach them well and let them lead the way ..." What are you teaching your child? What happens if they're not taught well? Remember, one day you may have to depend on them. If you haven't done your job as a parent, it will come back to you.

What does your attire say about your beliefs? When working, I always dress for success. If I were to greet a client in a pair of torn jeans and raggedy t-shirt and expect them to let me manage their money, do you think they'd trust me? Of course not! Your image is a part of who you are. It is a form of communication and can provide major insight into your personality or attitude.

One day I was about to do my radio show on building wealth for the retirement years. I was dressed in jeans and a t-shirt and felt so unprofessional that I raced home, dressed in my business attire and went back to the station where I nailed the show. My belief in dressing appropriately for business puts me in a strong and stable state of mind and that exudes its way across the airwaves to my future clients.

Even though no one could see what I was wearing, I still have this belief that I'm a stronger person when I dress for success. My confidence level rises immensely and I become a modern day Wonder Woman.

Marriage, rearing children, work ethics, morals, communication, friendships ... the list can go on. What are your beliefs in each of these and how strong is your foundation when it's weighed down in each category? What is your belief regarding money? Do you believe that the love of money is the root of all evil? Is this someone else's idea that you agreed with? What if someone loved money so much because it enabled them to purchase things for people that truly needed help? Would that change your belief that the love of money was the root of all evil?

I heard Anthony Robbins explain how a person could recognize what they truly believed in. To paraphrase him, he said, "A table top is the belief/foundation and the legs that hold it up are the support system to that belief."

Suppose your child thought he was a good baseball player, but wasn't quite sure. If you asked your child, "Can you field a grounder really well?" If he says yes, then that's one leg or one support of the foundation. "Can you hit the ball when you are at bat?" If he says yes, then he has a second leg that is supporting the belief/foundation. "Do you know the rules of the game and what's expected during any type of play?" Again, as he answers, he is building a structurally sound foundation. With the last question, he has four legs/pillars that enable him to know what he believes.

Finding your beliefs and not those of others is important to your foundation. When one's foundation is solid, rarely will they stumble or fall. When it does happen, it's usually because there was wrong information accepted as truth and without question. As an example from my past, when I met Mike, I was very superficial. I tried to build a family off an original thought of a nice ass and a cool car. Please someone tell me, is this any way to build a foundation? Of course not! The marriage was bound to fail because I'd accepted and built with material that wasn't based or strengthened by quality.

If I'd known how to recognize my beliefs, such as using the tabletop with support legs, I wouldn't have married Mike. I would have known he couldn't measure up to what I wanted in a man. That's how simple this information can be.

Do you follow or do you lead? Do you talk trash about people when they're not around? What do your actions tell others about you? As I said, write it out. Literally take a piece of paper and assign one task a week to figure out who you are and what you really believe in. You'll be amazed how your life will change once you know what you stand for. You know what they say, "If you don't stand for something, you'll fall for anything." Yes, that's a generalized statement, but just the same, find your foundation and if need be ... rebuild.

Wherever you are on the totem pole of life — rich, poor, happy, sad — there's a belief involved and it's dictating what you'll let yourself experience. Foundation and beliefs don't just appear, you build them throughout your life, one day at a time.

Chapter Fourteen

Business Views

Communication and Money

If you're self-employed in business, and you're not out to make big money, I have to ask, what are you doing? I'm not saying that one has to have a huge business or become greedy, but one should have a business that affords them the luxuries of life. I could have continued to work from my home and earn a good living, but by going the route I have, employing people, I'll eventually make a considerable amount more.

You give a little, and in return, you'll receive a lot. Remember when I said that I learned outflow equals inflow? Well, this works when you're advertising for more business, but it also works when you employ others. I'm outflowing an occupation to someone that needs to support themselves or their family, and in return, I not only feel good about this, but it allows my company to grow, which equals inflow. The more the business grows, the more jobs I can offer and that helps others to survive.

I believe there are some drawbacks to being too big in business, especially when you're running the whole show. I try to not micro-manage too much and I have learned that my key office personnel are worth twice their weight in gold (if not more).

I've often thought that the only reasons to be in business for yourself is, one, You're either tired of being told what you can or can't do (while employed by a company), or, two, you don't want your income to be limited by someone putting out less effort than you. Money does matter in life and when you're in business for yourself, it matters a whole lot more. You pay for your own insurance, you're never guaranteed a paycheck and if your business fails, then you're in serious jeopardy of losing everything you've worked for and own. For this last reason alone it means, once again, MONEY DOES MATTER!

Interesting thing about this last paragraph, I'm sure you've heard of all the people that lost everything they had during the recession. Well, being self-employed gives you an opportunity to continue to earn a living, even in the hardest of economic times.

I have a firm rule I adhere to and it's pretty simple —always be self-employed! I'll never punch a time card or answer to someone that isn't enhancing my life in some way. It's not that I can't take orders, but for me to be sub-servient to anyone is like pulling my own teeth ... it's not going to happen. I don't mind giving of myself in order to help others in need, but to be ordered around by anyone at any level of management makes my skin crawl.

You've read my story and have seen the TV show, so by now you should understand that I'm very protective of my integrity and I find it necessary to occasionally raise my voice when I feel I'm being wronged. I grew up watching my father lead and have learned that this is really the only way to get things done. If you want something, you have to speak up and lead the way.

I wanted a beautiful home for my family, a good edu-cation for my kids and a comfortable lifestyle for Donn and me when we retire. Though Donn is a very good provider, I'm acutely aware of what it will take to maintain what we've built. My point of view is that if I work hard while I'm still young, while I have the energy, then eventually the day will come when I can slow down and smell the roses. Right now, I'm plowing through the garden and continuously creating an optimal level of outflow.

Over the past three years my business has grown 70%. Being on the show helped tremendously, but I expect it to continue growing even after the final season. Why? Because I'm at the reigns and I have the drive to bring in the right people, make the right choices and steer this business in the direction that suits my purpose.

The biggest factor to my business point of view, the factor that helps me to grow the most, is communication. Nothing in the world gets done without a proper communication. Absolutely nothing! By keeping stats on my business and my employees, I instantly have information that tells me what's happening and where. When you're self-employed, communication has everything to do with how much money you will make.

A communication is not just telling someone that I want something. It's when I say what I want and then the same words are understood and repeated back to me. The conversation must go from Point A to Point B and back from Point B to Point A. The information going to and then coming back should not be altered. If a question does arise, creating added communication, it all gets sorted out until there is an A to B and B to A with no final alteration.

Any time there is a problem in any business, it is a communication problem. Regardless if it's human to human, human to machine, machine to machine, a problem can always be identified and repaired through proper communication.

Could you imagine having a great product that the world needs, but you didn't have anyone that could or would speak on its behalf? That product would sit on a shelf collecting dust until someone came along that understood communication.

Of course, the resolve would be to hire someone that knows how to communicate about the benefits of the product. Just note, if you're not the vocal type, there's nothing wrong with being the brains behind daily business operations and letting others engage the public with proper communication.

Personally, I'm fine with speaking about what I do. I believe in my product and its use in serving my purpose, my passion: making others safe. I believe that if you want to be successful at anything, there has to be passion coming from within. I've often had people tell me that they believe what I'm saying and can hear the passion in my voice. Why do you think they do that? It's because I'm on purpose and they, too, get excited.

Over the years I've met some very mild-mannered businessmen. Some of them have been extremely soft spoken. When talking with them, I'm amazed to find that they are so successful. Some have built large companies, or have been great investors, but what I have found in each of these successful people is not an overly cocky ego, but more so, an incredible confidence in what they do. They know their industry inside and out. They knew how to manage their money and use it to conquer and reach pinnacles.

When I speak with passion and someone hears it in my voice, they feel the confidence I exude. In turn, they become confident in me and know that I'm going to do right by them. Their money matters and they're instantly assured that I understand this.

As I covered in previous chapters, but would like to mention again in my business beliefs, are the main points that many people who are considered business savvy have. I'd also like to add that most anyone can decide to adopt these characteristics or knowledge for themselves.

Find your exact purpose: You will go much further in business if you truly know why you're doing it.

Know what your talent is: Your talent is a means to providing for your purpose.

Create Drive: Set a schedule and do exactly what needs to be done. Use a little tunnel vision and focus on results.

Passion: If people don't see or hear what you're passionate about, reconfirm with yourself what you're really about — not them, you.

Take Action: You can have all the drive you want, but if you're not known past the threshold of your door, you're not taking action.

Confidence: Know exactly who you are and what you do. If you don't know, learn! There is someone doing what you do. Find a successful mentor and become their shadow. Be willing to make and recognize your mistakes; this takes you closer to confidence.

Communication: Learn everything a communication is and is not. Any unresolved problem is a communication problem.

Statistics (Stats): The most important non-paid entity of your company. It tells you who the liars are and who is bringing in the gold. It has a direct relationship with communication. Together, they help you sustain your life — personal and business.

Money: It matters! Try existing without it. If you're always struggling when it comes to money, you have a communication problem. Usually that problem stems within you.

Confronting: Deal with each situation as quickly and professionally as it's presented.

This is what I believe in when it comes to business. Truly, there are not a lot of things one needs to worry about. If you handle each situation as it reveals itself, you'll stay ahead of the game. If you spend some serious time examining your business, your goals and fine tuning what you do, only then are you communicating.

Chapter Fifteen

Family Views

Where Families Have Gone Awry?

Don't get me started about family views. I don't consider myself to be the best mom in the world (though I try) and I could never accept the title of best wife, but I do have a point of view when it comes to family matters. I originate from the Northwest suburbs of Chicago, Illinois, where many of this country's immigrants settled. When these people of foreign lands came to the new world, they brought with them some very simple ideas and strong values.

They wanted to have a nice place where they could rear their children to be respectable in a society that offered the world, if they were willing to accept certain rules. The rules weren't hard to abide by: do your work and you'll receive your pay. Get out of line and you will pay the piper. Take care of your elders as they progress and need assistance.

I'm sure there were many more rules adhered to, but these basic ones, as I see it, are missing today. When I was a child, you understood that there were ramifications for bad behavior. We didn't have an abuse hotline we could call if Mom or Dad wouldn't buy us the cool pair of shoes or let our pants hang down to our knees. Yes, this is a bit of an exaggeration, but anyone in their 40s and above knows what I'm talking about. Belts, paddles, hangers, soap, rulers and sometimes a swift and solid hand were the tools used by the parents and understood by the children who chose to cross the line of authority.

Today, that line doesn't exist and I for one think it needs to come back into use. There seems to be very little respect from children today. I've seen elderly folks physically cut off or stumble because some skateboarder hasn't the sense or manners that dictate to be careful. There is no apology in the aft — "Excuse me, I'm sorry" — by the youth of today. I don't blame the kids so much as I blame the parents for not teaching the child etiquette or respect.

I've received quite a few positive comments over the years regarding my children, and how they're polite and respectful of others. This shows through their demeanor. I taught them that respect runs both ways, and that I had never better catch them being rude. When they were children, I used what was handed down through the generations ... soap or hot sauce. If either thought that they could be irresponsible by telling a lie or fighting with one another, they knew what the punishment would be.

I'm not "mommy dearest" by a long shot, but I do believe that as a parent, it's my responsibility to raise a child that will function well in a society, that I deem as tough. I believe that if a child doesn't learn at a young age the reasons for moral codes, then someone will eventually come along and teach them, one way or another. Truthfully, I'd rather them learn from me why manners and respect are so important, long before they get themselves into a situation with a stranger, through ignorance.

I've spoken with so many single parents over the years, mostly mothers trying to figure out what they can do to support their kids in the absence of a father figure. The best advice I can give them is to do everything in their power to raise their level of income and show their kids, by example, what it means to have integrity. This works for single mothers and fathers alike.

When I was just starting to date Donn, he was never allowed to sleep over. We didn't live together until after we married. What kind of message would I have been sending to Michael or Briana? It's amazing how some women don't understand what they're doing to the men and women of the future when they allow their boyfriend/girlfriend to live at their home with their children present. Knowing that one can up and leave at any moment sends a sign that there is no such thing as real commitment.

If a single mother of a boy or girl has multiple partners coming and going, the kids subconsciously learn that this kind of lifestyle is okay, it's acceptable. When your son is older and can't sustain a relationship because he's only seen men come and go throughout his life, you've become a major contributor as to why women can't find a man who will commit.

When a daughter is allowed to wear the trashiest or most revealing clothes, don't think for one minute that she's attracting the best of the male species. What message is being sent when a young girl wears sweats that say "Juicy" across the ass and she's only 13 years old?

Though I know it sounds like I'm longing for a perfect world, I'm not expecting one. At the same time, there is no reason one can give me for dropping their level of integrity just to join the masses and trying to be cool.

I know at this very moment, someone is saying, "Yeah, Vicki, but don't you do Botox? Don't you wear tops that reveal a little much?" My response is this: I do have some insecurities. I don't like the fact that I'm aging and will one day have wrinkles. Yes, I have had some work done here and there, so I keep up the good fight. As for my attire, I never reveal too much or too little. The way I dress is always age and occasion appropriate.

During a sermon, long ago, I learned from a pastor about marriage and holding a family together. Never play a game against your spouse. It's game over when you do. Cheating is playing the game against your spouse. Don't put yourself into a position where this can happen. Remember, if you can't tell everyone about what you're doing, perhaps you shouldn't be doing it.

Now-a-days it's so easy to quit a marriage. Back when I was with Mike, I truly didn't want to divorce, but through my parents having a good understanding of what was happening and then talking with me, I was able to sort things out and move onward. Divorcing Mike didn't instantly bring any happy thoughts and was more like watching a loved one from a distant boat as they were going down with the Titanic.

If one is considering divorce, I suggest you take a good look at what has really happened to the relationship. Could you, too, be at fault? Who started what and where? Where did the balance go? Who was not communicating? Not reciprocating to a spouse's desires is also a form of communication. You're telling them that it's your way or no way.

Any time you are not getting something from your spouse, regardless if its sex, conversations or any private time, something is going on in the game and you're not privy to it. This needs to change.

I believe when you take marriage vows, you really need to understand what you're getting into. A couple really should have a sense of each other and why they are with that person. As important as it is to know your spouse, one should also know themselves. What are your breaking points? Where do you draw the line on certain subjects?

Wouldn't it be interesting if every couple had to spend time with each other's ex-partners? How soon would the masks come off and reveal the true soul beneath? Truthfully, you don't even have to go to that length. Really, one just has to observe a potential spouse's home life, and over a period of months, listen carefully to the way they speak. Your partner will always tell you who they really are; you just have to be aware and not deny or make excuses for what you see or hear.

There would be a lot less divorces and children being dropped off or exchanged at the local McDonalds if people would just get over and fess up to their flaws and ill-fated judgments.

I've noticed that many people get divorced when the kids have grown. It's as if there is nothing left to the relationship and the party is over. I think it's a shame and sends a message to the world that marriage is just a farce. It's as if the vows aren't to be respected once the kids are grown. My God! This is the time that parents of grown kids should begin the real party. Create a new plan and start traveling together, take up yoga, skiing or whatever you can both enjoy. There was a time when couples had fun before the kids, so there's no reason they can't have even more fun after the kids. Keep creating a life that lets your kids respect what marriage is supposed to mean.

My mother and father had their share of arguments as have Donn and I. We don't just walk away from each other and find the nearest attorney because a few little incidents didn't go our way. Marriage can be tough and those that last are due to each person sharing in the responsibility of any problem. It takes a strong person to understand that the one they married has never been perfect, but so, too, they understand this of themselves.

When there is a better than 50% chance of marriages ending in divorce, it makes a statement about society as a whole. Not only does it make a sham out of the institution, but it tells you that love is based on conditions.

I believe there needs to be an understanding of the conditions so everyone in the game knows what to expect. If we're ever going to bring the divorce rate down, it's going to take a complete communication as to just how human we are and the foibles of which we are all capable of committing.

Though Donn, the kids and I don't go to church every weekend, the times we do have brought many reassuring thoughts to me regarding my marriage and relationships. Over the years I've heard that the church has been lacking in parishioner attendance. It makes me wonder if there is a connection to the divorce rate. I don't believe that one must go to church to be an upstanding citizen, but it can help a family to stay grounded and knowledgeable regarding the games they play or the paths they walk.

When we look out for our own personal gain more than what becomes of our family and friends, our actions dictate an ever-burgeoning downward spiral that will weigh down society as a whole. To know that I am just as responsible for this fact has made me stop to take notes on what I deem important and that I cannot just stand by and remain silent.

If I had a wish for the world regarding family life, it would be that you live in harmony, or at the least, if divorce is imminent, remain amicable and in complete communication, if for no other reason, the wellness of the future.

Chapter Sixteen

World Views

Why Aren't We Solvent?

I'm not declaring like Chicken Little that the sky is falling, but according to some of the country's best financial analysts, we're still heading for the 2nd great depression. With the unemployment rate higher than ever, over 200 banks having failed in a period of one year and a deficit that is truly unimaginable, one has to ask how much longer until the country will completely fold. The clock is ticking and if we're asking the right questions, then why aren't we going in the right direction for our sovereignty?

My parents were afraid for my generation and now I'm afraid for my kids. You've either seen, read or heard about this in the news, but I ask, what's really being done about the mess we're in? In my viewpoint, absolutely nothing!

Government officials are giving hand-outs like they're chocolate cupcakes at a nursery school. If we're broke, where is this money coming from? Let me tell you where. It's on the stroke of a keyboard like the one sitting in front of your PC. The Fed makes up money and loans it to the government. Sometimes, the government borrows from other countries, such as they've done with China. We owe so much money that we are barely making the interest payments. If you've ever had credit card debt you'll completely understand the major burden being pressed upon our children's children by our government.

Government officials are predicting that we'll be helping the Mid-eastern countries for the next 15 to 20 years. My question is why? We can't afford to be there, and truthfully, according to our founding fathers, we shouldn't be there. We're giving a handout instead of a hand up. It's time to let go and see if they can walk on their own. The only one that stays on a sinking ship is the Captain, so I'd like to know, why are we being asked by our officials to stay aboard?

We keep hearing how the bail-outs of the car companies was the right thing to do. If this economy continues to tank, how many of those cars will be repossessed. Better yet, why not let the car companies fail? I'm not a history major, but if history has taught us anything, when one company fails, another picks up the slack and becomes bigger through the loss of competition. It's near impossible to not hire more people as your company grows.

I believe the public leaders are leading us in the wrong direction. They don't have faith that people can and will figure out what to do for themselves. Failure, more times than not, breeds success. If a company doesn't create superior products, it will fail until it gets it right. Look at the Hyundai Automobile Company. In their beginning, they had the absolute worst reputation because their brand new cars were always breaking down. Today, they produce a sound and reliable automobile.

The misplaced workers from failed car companies could move to the new businesses springing up through the Green Movement. Think about all the new technology being developed that will need employees. I find it interesting that one of the biggest polluters of the world, the automobile, is in the throes of being rebuilt to suit the Green society. It's about time. As a matter of fact, this Green industry is creating so many jobs that there will be a shortage of personnel to keep up with demand. This, I believe, is where the bail-out money should have been going — to the future.

Though the government is throwing money to the Green sector, I believe it shouldn't have wasted one dime on the companies that have proven time after time to be mismanaged.

If you really want the economy to turn around, get rid of the Internal Revenue Service. Move to a consumer tax so illegal aliens and people that work under-the-table aren't exempt. Could you imagine what would happen if people came home with another $200-$500 a month in their paycheck? They'd begin to buy more things, clothing, meals, homes and cars. Imagine that, and all without the government being involved. One simple move, let people spend their money as they see fit ... all of their untaxed income dollars.

California is in a bind. For all the glorious sunshine we get, it has become an out-bound state. Companies and individuals are tired of being taxed on every little thing they do. Because the state's officials can't handle business correctly, they desperately work to push the problems onto the public through higher taxes or substantial business fines. This, again, is the wrong direction. Many states are now stealing businesses from California. They offer great incentives to move, and many companies have become more than happy to do so. If you can work from your home or have a business that is national, why would you stay for anything other than the sunshine?

I'm not a big follower of the political world, but I do know the effect the parties are having on our country. When you turn on the TV and see nothing but finger pointing coming from both camps, Democrats and Republicans, and you realize that neither side will ever agree on anything, it makes you wonder if that whole scene is the real "Reality" show.

Perhaps we should put some politicians in a house for three months and see how the public views them after the editors are done. Actually, I don't think the editors would have to do anything. The only time niceties occur in the political venue is when a politician is trying to get something that puts them in a good standing with the public.

"Where Clients are Family," is my company slogan. Who will be looking out for you when you need to retire? Certainly not the politicians.

I'll admit there was a time I was living with tunnel vision. I'd go to work, raise my kids, live another day and then do it all again. Today, as I'm getting older, I realize the ramifications of not paying attention to what my political leaders are doing. The policies they make have a direct affect on the livelihood of my retiring clients.

With so many laws changing constantly, I'm lucky to be connected to an industry that keeps me informed on what is taking place. I can take care of my clients, but also inform my mother what she should do regarding her retirement funds. There is so much confusion and misconception amongst retirees that they often don't know who they should be listening to or trust. It's incredible that we're asked to sock away funds for our retirements, yet the politicians have their own plan that allows them to collect from Social Security, but also continue collecting a major portion of their annual salary after retiring. Why are they receiving special compensation of taxpayers' money when they're no longer in office? We have to plan, but they don't. Hmmm!

So many people are still under the assumption that having their money in a 401k is still a safe bet. People think that their company plan is going to get them to retirement and everything is going to be fine, but it's not. People need to take action on their money now. In reality, the only person anyone should trust is themselves.

As stated, the country's brightest financial minds are predicting that we're really just at the tip of a big storm. You may have heard that we're coming out of the slump and the market is gaining strength. At times, it might seem that way, but as we all know, the numbers don't lie and neither do the great minds that are warning us. Make no mistake about this; we're going to have another ten years of a very turbulent financial crisis.

Think of this for one moment, "Our children's children are going to inherit our debt!" Does this statement claim that we are anywhere near resolve? No! It doesn't!

Over the next ten years I suggest that one should be conservative. Don't buy things you don't need and put the extra money in responsible places. Pay off your debt, your cars or any loans. Find the right financial tools that may not offer the biggest returns, but offer real safety while avoiding risk. If you can do it, work to make added payments on your home, to pay it off years ahead of time.

We've all seen where greed has taken this country. It's time to learn about your money and what it takes to keep the majority of it in your pocket.

I have this thought; if you're walking toward death's door (which we all are) and you don't want to die just yet, then perhaps you should walk the other way ... go the exact opposite direction of where you were heading. This is what I believe the world needs to do. Again, I'm not a history buff and I tend to focus more on the present and future, but after realizing the trillions of dollars spent to fight wars that haven't really benefited mankind, I ask ... for what are we forsaking our children?

I think we desperately need to change things in the political arena. Let's not worry so much on how some politician voted to go ahead with a war, but let's keep real statistics on each politician, and at the end of their term, really look to see if they've created a better society.

It's all in the stats ... the numbers don't lie.

MORE THAN A HOUSEWIFE

Chapter Seventeen

Women and Men

Same Traits, Different Gender

I haven't always been the best of friends with women. I have a core group from my past in Chicago, and a few here in Southern California, but really, I gravitate toward conversations with men and business.

I don't think most women understand me, other than those that are on the same page ... working to make things happen. When you see me on the show and these young women are asking questions like, "Why can't you do things with us during the day?" "Why are you always working?" "Why can't you take a break?"

Obviously, they don't understand the business I have and the money people have entrusted to me regarding their retirement and security. Many of these younger women today want to get married, have kids and let their husbands worry about making the money. I'm sorry, but my brain doesn't function that way, so not very many women friends in my circle.

One of the things I enjoy about my life is the business aspect. I truly get fulfillment and gratification knowing that I'm playing a very important role in the lives of many. To me, building a business is much more fun than sitting in front of the TV and watching soap operas. I rarely watch the tube and though it is a major part of my life in "reality," I believe it helps turn one's brain into mush (unless it's a documentary type of programming).

On The Real Housewives show, there is a lot of bickering between the women, and, to be honest, it has gotten rather ridiculous. When I started five years ago, it was fascinating to be on TV and to get recognized for some of my business achievements, but now when I watch the show and see how it was edited, it saddens me. I really can't believe some of my actions toward the other women, and for that matter, how they've reacted towards me.

In a time when women are gaining notoriety for their business acumen and making great strides in the public sectors, I feel like I'm slowing down the pace when I get into a ridiculous squabble over some trivial incident.

My goal, through this book and other venues, such as teaching women how to make money in the insurance industry, is to expand the role of women in the modern-day world.

I don't believe any woman should depend on a man for their livelihood. I understand the wants and desires of being a stay-at-home mom, but I highly suggest finding a home-based business where one can contribute to the lifestyle and needs of the family. This way, through self-employment, you can decide your hours of operation. If you need to pick up kids or run certain errands, you're able to do so.

Over the years, I've had a few disagreements with men on the show. Some either feel threatened by my income to theirs or because I tell their woman to find a job, create an income. My guess is that some men really like to have their wives 100% dependent upon them. The divorce rate has proven how well that works when the husband changes careers and fails, putting their lifestyle in complete jeopardy. Then there are the men who meet other women and proceed to walk away from their wife and kid(s). Yes, that even happens in Orange County to very beautiful women.

I believe women need to stop the bickering or trying

to one-up one another. "I've got bigger boobs." "I've got a smaller waist." "We have three Mercedes in our garage." We all know who has what and if you're using it to impress other women, I think you've got the wrong target. If I want to be appealing, it's for my man. Though I have gotten caught up in the bickering, and it's hard to regain control of my thoughts, I am tired of it.

I've taken up a new way of life lately. I jumped from a perfectly good airplane and I was in total fear. It was the most horribly frightening thing I'd ever done ... until I landed safely. I did it because I needed to. Okay, that's a lie. I did it out of much coercing. Now I can look back and understand how it works with my goals — I did something I really didn't want to do.

During an insurance bootcamp, I showed the film footage to a very large group of agents, many of whom were women. I told them, "If I can get the gumption to jump out of a perfectly good airplane, then you need to know what fears you can overcome." If you're a woman that is afraid of making cold calls, afraid of being alone, afraid that if you leave an abusive relationship you won't be able to make it on your own, then you need to find the trigger to those fears and confront them.

I'm seriously considering jumping out of another perfectly good airplane. Why? So I can show that when you do something a second time, you'll find that it's not so bad. You'll have proof that your original thoughts can be replaced at your will and that sometimes you need to do the things you think you don't want to do.

Yes, I thought it was a horribly frightening experience, until the shoot opened and I was floating down to earth. Although I was still nervous when approaching the ground, my jump partner confirmed that we were going to land one way or another, so we should probably do what was taught in the class.

An interesting thing happens when you use what you're taught; things seem to work out okay. Repetition takes away the fear and replaces it with confidence. If I did enough jumps, eventually it would be second nature to me, just like when I get on the phone for a cold call.

I also learned something about men while on the plane and heading to the jump zone. They too have fears and the need to overcome them. I've always wanted a forum to say this next statement, and this is as good of a place as any — I don't believe that anyone can separate the intelligence of male over female.

I've known some very ignorant men and some very ditzy women. I've also known some incredibly intelligent men and women. I don't believe anyone has a place-holder on intelligence, though I think men like to claim they're the smarter of the species.

I've heard it said that women can't make good decisions because they're more emotional than men. Then what of men who let their emotions run wild and begin hitting things in anger, or become impatient when they have no control? Do you see where this is going?

I think men and women need to understand each other in a more positive and intelligent way. The more we group each other as incompetent, the more damage we do, not only to each other, but to future generations.

Again, I have been guilty of doing those things I said we need to work on. I'm not separating myself from the problem, but I am trying to include myself as part of the solution.

If I could add anything to the game men and women play against each other, I'd want to say, that there needs to be a higher ethics level. Women: men often believe you're after them for their money. Men: ladies know that a "playful" innuendo is a play for "information." Women: there are plenty of good and available single men; leave the married ones alone. Men: same to you ... don't ask a married woman if she'd like to meet for dinner and drinks after a meeting (unless you're inviting a whole crowd along). These are just a few examples of the games we play against one another.

As a society we need to set our ethics and morals to a much higher standard.

As I speak, there is a huge women's empowerment movement happening. The more women get divorced or screwed over, the more they're going to say to themselves, "You know what, screw this! I'm not going to trust a man to get me where I need to be! I'm going to get there on my own!" I've received many emails from women telling me these exact words.

People want to change and if they feel as though they've been taken advantage of, then they will change the way they think and act, oftentimes proving they don't need anyone to help them get things done.

It's not hard to tell when someone has ulterior motives or is wearing a mask. With men or women, you can size them up by the way they talk. I can always tell if a man or woman has a high regard for ethics and morals. You can hear it in the way they speak. They don't make off-colored jokes, they don't put down their spouse and they avoid getting involved with people that do. I believe its called integrity.

The moral of this chapter is, don't get too comfortable. Life will be served up whether you're ready or not. We learn hard lessons from men and women on a daily basis and if you don't want the drama, keep your integrity in tow and move to a different venue.

Chapter Eighteen

Friendships

The Glue of Life

As kids, we grow up with friends surrounding us and they begin to know every little detail about our lives. Oftentimes, they'll remember distinct little things about you, which become the focal points for their view as to who you really are.

I was a popular girl in my youth. Then, something happened; I grew up, graduated high school and my friends went this way and that. I felt I was left to wander in limbo, not knowing if I was considered a kid or an adult. Though I still hold my past friendships close to my heart, people who kept me centered and made up a distinct part of who I am, I realize that I've grown, created new friendships, and have established myself in an adult world where solid friendships don't come as easy as they did in my youth.

When people take information they think they know of me and hold me captive to their thoughts, they not only shortchange me, but also themselves.

My friends in Southern California haven't shared the experiences of my youth such as my friends in Chicago. My lifelong friends grasp exactly why I do certain things or have an attitude about a given situation; I'll never be so far removed from the person they knew back when. They accept that's the way I am and know it's the way I've always been.

My Mid-west friends don't shut me off if they're not happy with something I've done. My friends here on the West Coast often shortchange me by not knowing or addressing the fact that I'm not much different than I was as a kid; just a bit more driven and secure in myself.

Because these new friends haven't taken the time to know the lifetime of me, they're quick to look for friendships elsewhere.

A person can create friendships wherever they live and whatever their age, but until the depths of a new found friend are completely explored, one will never grasp what makes up the person they call their friend. So judgment of character should be held at a minimum. If you're looking for a friend that believes only as you do, you're not looking for a friend, but a clone.

Though it was never directly pointed out, I've learned through watching the show what real friendship should mean. The show depends upon gossip and confrontations, and each week I get the opportunity to see what it takes to be friends with someone. Real friends adjust through conflicts. When a friend's history is readily available for your examination, take the time to learn about them and not rush to judgment. The results may not always be satisfactory to the parties involved, but they should be on the table and exposed for each other to grasp what is affecting one or the other.

One needs to be able to depend upon a friend during difficult times. Holding special information as confidential is imperative not only to the one experiencing difficulties, but also for your integrity as well. Every time we speak behind a friend's back, are we really being a friend? I don't think so. We're compromising our own integrity.

Regardless if we are sharing what we believe to be the truth about someone, it can still be hurtful and possibly slanderous — doing absolutely no good for either party.

I thought about exposing more on my first marriage, but decided against it. The marriage is over and has been for a long time. It doesn't take a rocket scientist to realize that something went wrong, became unbalanced. As stated previously, "Anytime there is a problem that goes unresolved, it's a communication problem."

We've all heard about the power of association; our personal or business friends are a tell-tale sign of how others will view us. Fashion, career and even religion are small portholes to help someone determine if they want to be your friend.

Are you involved with people who are searching for answers in life? Are you involved with friends that are progressive and ethical? Though I don't suggest ever dropping a real or lifelong friend, there comes a time when you have to do what is right for you. When you listen to how a friend expresses their thoughts, you'll know if you want to remain in the picture. If you remain close to a friend that is constantly negative, through the power of association, you too may become or be seen as negative. Do you want this in your life? Through comments from viewers I've learned that I'm an associate to negativity and this bothers me.

If you don't have any solid friendships, you need to ask yourself, why? What are you doing or what have you done to isolate yourself from people. In this regard, you have a person-to-person communication problem, but the first person you should be thinking about is yourself.

Having people to socialize with and having real friendships are two very different things. Real friends will invite you to dinner, a get-together or other events. A socializing friendship is one where you think you know what's going on with someone, but you really know very little. This kind of friend is usually just about the weather, sport scores or the superficialities of daily living and often happens around a local bar with a lot of other lonely people. As the song goes from the TV sitcom Cheers, "You want to go where everybody knows your name." We all want friends and will find them wherever we can.

True friendships are hard to come by, and so easily

destroyed by gossip. Slander is oftentimes a daily occurrence, yet we rarely recognize we're doing it. Until someone slaps a lawsuit against you, are you willing to recognize how simple one passes defaming information? This pitifully simple form of speaking that so many habitually do on a daily basis can devastate a life and a career. An apology may help, but it would have to be so sincere, and then accepted from the recipient of the offense. From that point, one would have to dig really deep into their own affairs and learn the real reasons they would make a judgment against another in the first place.

Facts that can be proven beyond a shadow of doubt in court or through legal records are not defaming, but a moment of history preserved for one's integrity. We can learn of ourselves by the accusations of others.

There is a thought about unconditional love. We readily see it on the news when a parent stands by their child who is guilty beyond a shadow of a doubt. It's not wrong for this parent to continue to love their child, nor is it wrong for them to continue to stand by their side. Doing so doesn't mean that the parent agrees with what the child has done, but more so, that they want the child to know that even through the bad, there is still someone that cares about them.

How unconditional are we with our friends? How quick does one want to wash their hands of any connection to the source of malicious or bad deeds? Most often, it's right away. It's when we can stand back and absorb the human condition, the erring side of life, and admit to ourselves that we're as vulnerable to mistakes and offensive accusations as others, that we can literally see how fortunate we are to not have blundered in our own, sometimes despiteful, ways.

Friendships are oftentimes filled with conditions and I think it does need to be that way. One may have a condition that, "if you treat me this way, I will be gone." Another may have a condition that, "if you treat me this way, we

190

will discuss it, and if nothing changes in your thoughts or actions to better our situation, I will be gone." There is an agreement, a condition on what is acceptable between two parties. Being unconditional is a nice thought, but in reality, human beings experience things throughout their lives and will never be able to completely escape a past emotion that contributes to conditions.

It seems a bit reversed, but it's tough to be unconditional with friends as compared to a spouse or your family. With friends, you just expect them to know better, even if they truly don't. Yet, with family, you don't always care if they know better, you've grown up used to their idiosyncrasies; we've heard them throughout our lives and believe that it's just the way they are and always will be. I've met a few people over the years that have cut family members completely out of their lives; they set a condition and stuck to it. Is this wrong to do? I can't say. It's not the choice I would make, but I'm not them.

It's been said, "In the end, family is all you have." I agree. I know that my siblings and I get along rather well. Though we're 3,000 miles apart, we have an unconditional love. At times we lash out, yet there's still a bond that says, I accept you as you are, flaws and all.

If we could just learn to do this with any of our friendships, we would be in a much better place with the world when it's time to leave.

There is so much more that could be expressed about friendships, and if I could suggest anything, it would be that you knock on the door of any friend you've had a past disagreement or temporarily lost contact with and offer them not only your hand, but a hug. After all, we are not complete as human beings without friendships.

MORE THAN A HOUSEWIFE

Chapter Nineteen

Maturing a Life

Completing My Puzzle

Throughout our lives we should be growing mentally stronger and stable. There've been many times that I would stop to wonder what I was doing with my life. I'm not talking about my purpose or my business, so much as just the idea of growing up.

I labeled the first section, "Transformations," and the first chapter began with where I thought the real meat of my life started, my childhood. When I look back on everything I've talked about in this book, and other things I may not have mentioned, it's now I realize how far I've come, yet how much further I must travel.

As a child, I had a very comfortable family life and even though I went through the operations for Cholesteatoma, I still somehow knew that I was going to be all right. Perhaps it was the tunnel vision I lived with.

I know that there are many men and women in the world that have had an extremely hard life. I could never compare my existence to theirs. It just wouldn't be right for me to even try.

If there were any words of wisdom that I could share with those experiencing a hardship, it would be for them to take a really clear and concise look at their life, their past. Whatever your age is at this moment, think about how you've made it to this point. You've survived by your will, your determination to get through. You may have experienced the worst of the worst and yet you're still here. Hopefully, you're able to understand that you made it through what others may not have been able to cope with for one single moment.

It's when we throw our hands in the air and quit, that life gets really difficult. That's when we accept failure and I personally never want to admit that I just can't continue.

When I realize how many bumps I ran into on my journey thus far, all of those muddy roads, I know that there will be more to come. I accept these bumps and bruises as a part of what has built my character. I thank the man above that I have only gone through minor childhood issues and that I haven't experienced anything so tragic that my spirit would be completely broken.

Though I didn't know it at the time, I made it through my teen years without any super heavy hitches, at least none that matter to me now. As I jumped the hurdles in life, sometimes unknowingly, I built an internal encyclopedia of what I should and should not do. Does this information really help me throughout my life? This is just one of the questions I ponder.

When I speak of aging and getting mentally stronger and stable, I'm talking about the realization that I've made it this far and have done pretty damn good. I reassure myself ahead of time that any future bumps coming my way will be confronted and challenged without hesitation.

The more we understand our transformations throughout our lives, the calmer we should become. Some people choose to throw their hands in the air and let God take over, while at the same time, continuing to work and support their families. I've never been a practitioner of this method, but there have been times I've truly wanted to. It's then that I think perhaps God doesn't want me to slow down, that there are people who I can help through my service, my purpose.

Working through my first marriage taught me to not stand still and let other people make the very important decisions concerning my life. Though Donn is the man I truly love, even through the hardest of times, I know I still have some growing to do. I need to become a wife that can let go of the reigns, or at the minimum, share them more willingly.

Donn really is the most patient man I've ever met and his integrity, though I haven't spoken much about it, is of the highest quality and assures me that someone as strong as him can care for someone not so perfect, such as me. In that respect, he reminds me of my father and what a real man should be.

The TV show has been a very big instigator to understanding what I need to work on concerning my personality and reactions when life serves something I may not want or like. I've learned that every time an emotion is displayed — anger, sadness, hatred, apathy, or even happiness and laughter — it's a signal that I'm being triggered to something from my past.

It's when we can find the root of that emotion in our past that we become less controlled by it. Unfortunately, I am oftentimes moving at lightning speed, and when I get triggered, I tend to speak before I really think. I let the opportunity pass me by. So, when I speak of maturing, it's in this arena that I know I must do the most work. Having a sharp tongue is never a good tool to use when a trigger has been released, but a sharp mind is a mature person's best chance to a peaceful existence.

When it comes to business, I know there are many things I will be doing that I haven't thought of yet. For instance, this book was an eye opener. Through many hours of being questioned and breaking down my thoughts, I've furthered my education into the inner world of my mind. I wanted everything revealed to be of a positive nature, but I also understood that if I want to help others achieve success in life, I must first admit my own faults, how I handled them, and teach through example.

Through my business, I have had to relearn how to deal with others in an office environment. When you've worked alone for as long as I had, depending on only yourself for your business needs, and then you're sharing an office with employees and must wait while someone else handles what you were used to doing quickly, I admit, it takes some real getting used to. I don't know if I'll ever be completely comfortable with someone doing a job in 20 minutes that I think I could have done in 10. I guess that's something I need to learn to let go of.

Is there ever a real measure of maturity? I've seen some older folks that still get perturbed about this or that. I know I would like to be so comfortably set when I retire, that absolutely nothing can bother me. Is that really possible? I guess only time will tell.

I want to thank you for reading my book and if you'd like to make a comment you can email me through either website listed below.

If you see me out on the town somewhere, don't be afraid to wave, say hello or even to give your best shout out... Woo-hoo!

Take care and thanks for everything,

Vicki G.

www.morethanahousewifebook.com
www.vickigunvalson.com

FRIENDSHIPS

The next section is for those who would like to consider
a career in the insurance industry.
It is a short platform from which you can learn
the basics of what it takes to become an
agent for Coto Insurance.

Section Five

Entrepreneurs

Chapter Twenty

Coto Insurance

Becoming an Agent

Insurance is absolutely one of the biggest industries in the world, bar none. The game, should you decide to play, is to realize the potential benefits, not only for the client, but also for your lifestyle.

The home you live in, the car you drive, the doctor you visit, the business you work for, the dentist that keeps your teeth pearly white, are all covered by insurance in one way or another. Should I not mention the coverage on one's life? To be completely honest and factual about this one area of coverage, it is the one bet that is undeniably, 100% proven to be a guaranteed return on the dollar. Everyone at some point in time is going to die.

I know this could sound morbid to some and I don't like bringing up the thought of a loved one, or for that matter, ourselves ... dying, but it is inevitable.

When I first started out, I saw this industry as a way to provide for my children and me. Later on, as I figured out what my purpose was and how I was already doing it, things began to make more sense. I've always been concerned for the welfare of others whether it was about creating and sharing memories or just making sure they were safe.

The first time I hand delivered a check to a woman that had lost her husband, and father to their kids, I knew I was in the right business. It hadn't been long from the point I'd sold the policy that an unfortunate chain of events occurred. It truly felt so good to know that this family was going to be financially secure.

Some agents may never get to experience this type of feeling — an overwhelming rush that makes you take a deep breath and know you truly did right by this family.

Whether you're already a licensed agent that is looking to expand your business, would like to move from an existing office, create your own web-based business or perhaps you're someone that wants more information on how to become an agent, then please, bear with me as we go over a few steps to consider.

(The following information is for those that are not licensed insurance agents. If you are already an agent and would like to know more about working with Coto Insurance, then please read the last page of this chapter or visit our website at www.cotoinsurance.com)

In order to become a life insurance agent, most states require you to fulfill a certain number of pre-licensing hours. There are classes you can attend in either a classroom setting or Online (through the Internet). Depending upon who you go through, your course and licensing fees may vary from $200 to $400.

After putting in the classroom/online time, roughly 52 hours, you will qualify for a licensing test which is governed by your state.

Once you have your home state license we'd like to talk with you regarding a great start to your career. We have all the tools necessary for success and no matter where in the U.S. you're located, we can help.

Even insurance agents need to have insurance and this comes in the way of "E & O" which stands for "Errors and Omissions." This is a type of insurance that covers you, the agent, for liability. In order to do business or to be contracted with the insurance carriers, they will require this coverage. It covers you for any errors that you may commit while representing the client. If you were to give a client some information that wasn't factual or turned out to damage them somehow, this insurance would cover you in the case of a lawsuit. The price for E & O is usually $400-$950 annually. Don't let the cost of this discourage you. Though it's required, it really is a small price to pay for peace of mind.

Since the Patriot Act was enacted there is training for Anti-Money Laundering (AML) and takes roughly 45 minutes to complete. Literally, everyone in a line of work which regards the Financial Services Industry must complete this training.

Pretty simple thus far, right? Don't get overwhelmed by any of this. I can tell you from experience, it's not that difficult. Even though I didn't know anything about all of the above... AML, E & O, 50+ hours of class, or even how to sell by using a phone, I didn't bother with any of that. I just took one step at a time and got my license first.

If I were to suggest anything to you at this moment, it would be to not only get your life & health insurance license. In some states they offer, Life, Accident and Health. If you get more than one license then you're able to increase your income by having the ability to sell more than one type of policy.

For complete information about the insurance industry, you can Google "CA Department of Insurance" or " Department of Insurance" (Using your state instead of CA.)

To get your insurance classes completed through an Online/Internet access please go to: www.ableincorporated.com/clp/R0F45ECFFCA4.aspx

Again, call us when you've received your license and we will email you exact instructions on how to obtain your E & O insurance and complete your AML training. Then, if you choose to become a member of the Coto Insurance team, we can help guide you through the steps it takes to learn phone sales techniques, purchasing Exclusive or Shared leads or receive training by established online sales veterans.

You will be working for yourself as a sole proprietor with your own company name. Eventually, as you build your business you'll want to incorporate. Your commission checks come directly from the insurance companies and are deposited right into your account every time a policy is issued, placed and paid.

If you choose to work with COTO VIRTUAL ALISS Software the cost of use is $60 monthly. There is also a COTO ALISS training fee of $199. This includes hands-on training with top producers. Any agent placing $25,000 of premium (within 12 months of training) will get $174 of the training fee refunded.

Starting a business in insurance isn't cheap, but if you really think about it, the expense is nothing compared to what you can make. Here is a really quick bullet list.

Getting licensed	$200 - $400
Errors & Omissions	$400 - $950 (annual)
2 or more out-of-state licenses	$50 - $300
Coto Training Manual	$395 (optional)
Exclusive/Shared Leads*	$700 - $1400*
Doing Business As (DBA)	$50 - $250 (license)
Office Phone or VOIP*	$35 - $150 (monthly)
Coto ALISS Software	$60 (monthly)
Coto ALISS Training	$199

While there may be some other expense that we don't cover here, such as the rent on your home, or your monthly expenses, I just wanted to show you the basics.

If you added up the highest dollar amount on each of these, you'd see that you would pay closer to $4000 to start a business of your own. Most of those bullet items are a one-time-only fee or an optional fee. Those items that are monthly are nominal when you think about it.

Even if you kept your day job and worked at selling insurance in the evening through your leads list, you could take your time building a solid foundation and focus on becoming a real professional insurance agent. You don't need a fancy office or a pricey car. Most sales will be over the phone and those that aren't will oftentimes be through someone nearby that you've been referred to.

Assuming that you already have a computer, VOIP* and other basic office tools, then getting started is just a few clicks away. Actually, come visit the Coto Insurance site at www.cotoinsurance.com and learn as much as you can. If you have further questions, just leave an email message and we will respond to any serious inquiries.

* LEADS – Exclusive Leads are your biggest expense. You need to budget $700-$1400 the first 2 months and then $2000/mo thereafter for Exclusive Leads. More, if your goals are greater. I believe most agents would agree that this cost is nominal compared to the return on investment.
You may choose to purchase Shared Leads which are considerably less but you're competing with several other agents on each lead. When first starting out, you may want to use shared leads or a combination of Exclusive and Shared Leads.

*VOIP – Voice Over Internet Protocol. You've seen people talking with a headset on in front of their computer. Oftentimes this is because they are using the internet and not a landline phone.

Coto Insurance is waiting to hear from you. Here are a few reasons to team with us:

Coto offers a low cost, modern business opportunity.

Coto has state-of-the-art tools – Coto ALISS – (Automated Life Insurance Selling System)

COTO has the best training in the business, from established online sales veterans.

COTO has the best leads in the business – bar none!

COTO has quality people to help push your cases

through underwriting and get you paid!

With all the advantages COTO has to offer, why trust your future insurance sales career to anyone else!

There are many more things I could tell you regarding the insurance industry and its rewards, but I'd rather meet you in person one day ... perhaps at one of Coto's motivational bootcamps or cruises.

There are many people out there that need an income and may be afraid to step across a boundary they've set up for themselves. If this is you or someone you know, I'd really like to assure you that you can make the move to a better future. I didn't invent the insurance industry. There was a time that I was unsure, but also, I was curious and took the step to see.

I hope you consider the offer and give yourself the opportunity to be successful in this industry. Listed below are a few of the webinars we offer to help you see exactly how the pros do it. When you duplicate what others do, it really just becomes a numbers game. How many times you can pick up that phone in a day is the only thing you'll have to ask yourself.

ALISS Sales Training
This webinar allows you to be a "fly on the wall" as you listen and watch top producer, trainer and mentor Barry Molloy make LIVE, un-screened, un-rehearsed sales phone calls to exclusive life insurance leads from Efinancial. You'll hear his live conversations and see every move of his mouse, as he uses the ALISS system to sell life insurance to real prospects over the telephone. Whether you have years of experience selling over the phone, or are considering selling life insurance over the phone for the first time, you'll benefit from this webinar! You'll see the entire sales process from breaking the ice to closing the sale, taking the application and scheduling the paramed exam. In addition, the last 30 minutes of the webinar are reserved for live

Q&A. (Approximately 2.5 hours)

ALISS 101
This webinar will address the needs and most frequently asked questions of the new ALISS user. You'll learn all about: working with and entering prospects into ALISS; the importance of gathering accurate health history; the effect of certain medications, family history and the use of nicotine products, other than cigarettes, on the prospect's underwriting rate classification. You'll also learn: how to run rated quotes; take and complete automated applications in real time on ALISS; the importance of, and how to pre-set paramed exams; as well as how to utilize ALISS to make sales calls, track your sales results, and schedule follow-ups so you get the most from each and every life insurance prospect. (Approximately 90 minutes.)

ALISS 102
Designed for the intermediate to advanced CSS user, this webinar will address your needs, and answer your questions about: using the Tools and Work tabs; getting the most from the ALISS Work Summary, the To-Call, To-Do, and Underwriting Information lists and functions. You'll see what the experts do to get the most from the Prospect screen, and discover all the secret ins and outs of the Pending, History and Case Management tabs. You'll also learn how to use all four (4) phases of the Sales Cycle to your maximum benefit, and how to move your prospects from Application-Out to Underwriting. (Approximately 90 minutes.)

Instant Issue Product Training
Is the prospect in a hurry, afraid of needles, or just "not worth the time" full-underwriting takes? Fidelity Life offers a solution that combines the strengths of electronic no-needle underwriting with the judgment of real live underwriters. The result is term insurance to $300,000 without an

exam, or proof of mortgage, that can issue in 48 to 72 hours. This live training takes you through writing a non-med policy application. Fidelity offers you the choice of either a paper, or completely electronic life insurance application. You'll learn how to take both, as well as get an e-signature, Social Security number, and payment information from your prospect. You'll see how to submit the application and get it put in-force quickly, and track the policy through from application to place paid! Fidelity provides a great way to get some cash flowing quickly! (Approximately 1 hour.)

Getting the Signed Application
Back & Through Underwriting
This webinar covers a subject which is as important as writing the deal, namely: Getting the signed application back! It's been said that taking the app is the beginning of the sale, and that getting the application back is the critical step in getting the application into underwriting, so it can be approved, delivered, placed, paid, and put in force. You'll see how to use ALISS' automated technology to track the applications you have written in ALISS, utilize the ALISS automation engine to keep you in constant contact with your applicants, hear live calls to real life insurance applicants, and the fine points that increase the odds of getting the life applications back in a timely manner. Don't miss this important how-to course. (Approximately 1 hour.) Training Cost is $199.00 for one month of access. These courses are included in your COTO-ALISS sign-up fee. $174.00 of your access fee will be refunded if you achieve $25,000 placed and paid business within the first twelve months of completing the training

As stated, once you learn, step by step, our process for success, you'll be on your way to a brighter future. Make the decision to join us today.

(For those of you that are already agents please read below)

If you are already a licensed life and health insurance agent and have been struggling with how to make a living in insurance sales, you have come to the right place. I have a proven lead generation system that will allow you to sell term life insurance right from your office. No more driving around spending money on gas and time away from your office.

The ALISS system, which is part of the Coto Insurance & Financial Services team, is one-of-a-kind. It is the sole reason for my success.

Coto Insurance & Financial Services is a full-service life insurance brokerage agency. We are committed to providing agents with:

Top commissions

Lead option programs available

A patent-pending automated sales system: "ALISS"

Please register at our website **www.cotoinsurance.com**

We wish you success in your business and look forward to hearing from you!

www.cotoinsurance.com

Jeff Scott is located in Southern California and ghostwrites for business professionals, copywrites for companies and authors his own material under self-help fiction.

He can be contacted at jscott@tdoent.com.

MORE THAN A HOUSEWIFE

The Palatine House

My Parents

213

Coto Insurance Office

Kathy, Vicki, Mom, Billy, Lisa, and Kim

My Home Office

MORE THAN A HOUSEWIFE